Stag and Doe
Bed and Breakfast

Stag and Doe Bed and Breakfast

Mark Crawford

Stag and Doe and *Bed and Breakfast*
first published 2015 by
Scirocco Drama
An imprint of J. Gordon Shillingford Publishing Inc.
© 2015 Mark Crawford

Scirocco Drama Editor: Glenda MacFarlane
Cover design by Terry Gallagher/Doowah Design Inc.
Author photo by Liz Beddall
Printed and bound in Canada.

We acknowledge the financial support of the Manitoba Arts Council and The Canada Council for the Arts for our publishing program.

All rights reserved. No part of this book may be reproduced, for any reason, by any means, without the permission of the publisher. This play is fully protected under the copyright laws of Canada and all other countries of the Copyright Union and is subject to royalty. Changes to the text are expressly forbidden without written consent of the author. Rights to produce, film, record in whole or in part, in any medium or in any language, by any group, amateur or professional, are retained by the author.
Production inquiries should be addressed to:
Playwrights Guild of Canada
401 Richmond Street West, Suite 350
Toronto, ON M5V 3A8
Phone 416-703-0201
Fax 416-703-0059
info@playwrightsguild.ca

Library and Archives Canada Cataloguing in Publication

Crawford, Mark, 1981-, author
  Stag and doe ; Bed and breakfast / Mark Crawford. -- 1st edition.

Plays.
Contents: Stag and doe -- Bed and breakfast.
ISBN 978-1-927922-17-0 (paperback)

  I. Crawford, Mark, 1981- Bed and Breakfast. II. Title.

PS8605.R435S73 2015   C812'.6   C2015-906096-6

J. Gordon Shillingford Publishing
P.O. Box 86, RPO Corydon Avenue, Winnipeg, MB Canada R3M 3S3

For my family:
immediate, extended, chosen, and yet-to-come.

Acknowledgments

I acknowledge and appreciate the support of the Ontario Arts Council's Theatre Creator's Reserve. Through this program, *Stag and Doe* received recommendations from Port Stanley Festival Theatre and The Grand Theatre, and *Bed and Breakfast* from Thousand Islands Playhouse, Festival Players of Prince Edward County, and Port Stanley Festival Theatre.

For *Stag and Doe*, I'd like to thank Marion de Vries, Deb Sholdice, Simon Joynes, Melissa Kempf, and all the actors who participated in workshop readings, especially those who read an early draft during a torrential downpour in exchange for pizza and beer. And my very deep gratitude to Miles Potter for bringing his insight, intelligence, and brilliant sense of humour to the development and direction of this play.

Bed and Breakfast was developed as part the Thousand Islands Playhouse Playwrights' Unit. Many thanks to the other unit members (Attila Clemann, Jodi Essery, Paul Van Dyck, and Rona Waddington) for their invaluable input. Thanks also to Brett Christopher, Charlotte Gowdy, and Richard Van Dusen. I'm enormously grateful to Ashlie Corcoran for her belief in this play from the beginning, and for her artistry, vision, and joy in bringing it to the stage.

For both plays, I thank the hugely talented casts, designers, stage managers, production teams, and staff at both the Blyth Festival and the Thousand Islands Playhouse for their diligence and dedication to the premiere productions of these two plays.

Thanks also to the Playwrights' Guild of Canada; to Gordon Shillingford, Glenda MacFarlane, and everyone at Scirocco Drama; to Gil Garratt for acting as my playwriting doula; and to Paul Dunn for his unwavering patience and support.

Playwright's Note

Stag and Doe and *Bed and Breakfast* are both set in pretty specific locations in Ontario, but they are both about some pretty universal stuff. Part of the fun for an audience is in recognizing their world on stage. And part of the power is the way in which that recognition implicates them in the events and the ideas.

While I have no interest in rewriting *Stag and Doe* or *Bed and Breakfast* to set them in Anytown, North America, I am open to adjusting references for future productions. For example: if your audience doesn't know what the LCBO is, we could easily change it to "Liquor Store". Or if they're not familiar with Kathleen Wynne, we could replace her with another notable lesbian. This is not an invitation to make changes to the text without my permission; it's an acknowledgment that the audience's frame of reference and regional jargon isn't the same everywhere you go…and won't be the same as time goes along.

In the spirit of including your audience in the world of the play and holding that old mirror up to nature, feel free to get in touch with me through the Playwrights Guild of Canada. Let's chat!

Mark Crawford

Mark Crawford's first play, *Stag and Doe*, premiered at the Blyth Festival in 2014 and has received multiple subsequent productions. His second play, *Bed and Breakfast*, premiered in 2015 at the Thousand Islands Playhouse. As an actor, Mark has performed at theatres across Canada. Mark grew up on his family's beef farm near Glencoe, Ontario. A graduate of the University of Toronto and Sheridan College, he now lives in Toronto.

Stag and Doe

Production History

Stag and Doe premiered at the Blyth Festival in the summer of 2014 with the following cast:

BONNIE	Elizabeth Kalles
DEE	Rebecca Auerbach
BRAD	Eli Ham
MANDY	Nicole Joy-Fraser
ROB	Jason Chesworth
JAY	Greg Gale

Directed by Miles Potter
Set Design by Pat Flood
Costume Design by Alison Marshall
Lighting Design by Steve Lucas
Sound Design by Todd Charlton
Stage Manager: Crystal MacDonnell
Assistant Stage Manager: Heather Thompson

A few weeks later, a second production of *Stag and Doe* opened at Port Stanley Festival Theatre with the following cast:

BONNIE	Sarah English
DEE	Kate Gordon
BRAD	Matthew Gorman
MANDY	Rose Napoli
ROB	Jaron Francis
JAY	Mark Crawford

Directed by Simon Joynes
Set Design by Eric Bunnell
Costume Design by Alex Amini
Lighting Design by Darryl Crichton
Sound Design by Travis Hatt and Simon Joynes
Stage Manager: Lani Martel
Assistant Stage Manager: Joseph Recchia

Characters

BONNIE, the doe
DEE, her best friend
BRAD, the stag
MANDY, a bride
ROB, her groom
JAY, a chef
All characters are in their mid-twenties to early thirties.

Setting

The kitchen of a reception hall in a small town in Southwestern Ontario. It's the kind of all-purpose community hall where you'd have your 4-H banquet, your Stag and Doe, your wedding reception, and your fiftieth wedding anniversary party. This building was erected in the heyday of these community halls: sometime between the late fifties and mid seventies. The place is of an era and its contents are a hodgepodge of every period since it was built. It's still a busy reception hall for events like those in the play, but it's probably seen better days.

There is an out-of-date industrial stove, or two mismatched residential ranges side-by-side. There are a couple of refrigerators, or a fridge and a chest freezer. There's a big double sink and a large kitchen island with a stool or two. There are four entrances and exits: the back door of building, a double-swing door that goes directly into the reception hall, a door or corridor that leads to the rest of the building (the front door, lobby, and washrooms), and this being a comedy, there is a door to a storage closet.

Time

The present. A Saturday in June. The play takes place over the course of one day.

A Note on Sound

Sound is used to establish and maintain the reality of the world outside this kitchen. This starts at the end of Act I with some wedding guests arriving and continues for the rest of the play, underscoring the entirety of Act II. It's important to have well-placed speakers, believable (and variable) party sounds, a great music playlist, and a bump in volume every time the swinging door opens. The constant rumble of the party provides yet another obstacle for the actors and keeps the pressures of the event alive for them and for the audience.

Act I

Scene One

It's 10:30 in the morning on a Saturday in June. Lights up to reveal BONNIE. She is alone on stage, but the door to the storage closet is open. She's reading the back of a Jell-o box out loud.

BONNIE: "Stir one cup boiling water into jelly powder. Stir until completely dissolved. Stir in one cup cold water. Chill until set." It just gives me the regular recipe for making Jell-o, it doesn't say how much booze to put in.

DEE: *(Appearing from the storage closet holding a game.)* Yeah, I don't think it's going to tell you that on the box.

BONNIE: Well, it should! You know, my grandma always used this to make that Jell-o mould with the grated carrot she took to potlucks, and my mom just made Jell-o when I was sick, but I think the only time I've ever bought it is to make shooters. What does that say about me?

DEE: You're no good at a potluck or around sick children, but you know how to have a good time.

BONNIE: So what do I do? Just substitute booze for water?

DEE: Professionally, I can't really recommend that.

BONNIE: Thank you, Nurse Dee. Seriously, how do I make them?

DEE: It's two parts boiling water, one part cold, one part booze. And it works better if the liquor's cold too, like if you keep the bottles in the freezer over night.

BONNIE: Well, that's not going to happen now. Brad was going to the LCBO when they opened—he should be here by now.

DEE: What time is it?

BONNIE: *(Checking her cell phone for the time.)* 10:33.

DEE: We're cutting it close. OK, when Bradley gets here, we get these made and in the fridge STAT. Remember this, Bonnie: Jell-o is like a man—you put enough booze in there, it takes a hell of a lot longer to get hard. Did you decide on the prices for these?

> *She's referring to the ring toss, the mini-putt, and the roulette wheel she's hauling out of the closet. The games are a mix of homemade and store bought, new and old.*

BONNIE: I was thinking you'd get one turn for a loonie and three turns for five bucks.

DEE: So, the price goes up the more you play?

BONNIE: Oh, wait. I think I meant that the other way around.

DEE: You really are a genius with the numbers these days.

BONNIE: Shut up.

DEE: So...how did Brad take the news?

BONNIE: None of your business. What do most people charge?

DEE: Well, it used to be one turn for a loonie and three

for a toonie. But everything changed around the time of Becky Walsh and Greg Wasileski's Stag and Doe—they were having that destination wedding in Cuba, so they figured they could jack up the prices and people would understand. I was a bit like, "Hey Becky! I hope you have a good time getting married on the beach in the middle of January, but why the hell am I paying for it?" I want to go to an all-inclusive as much as the next girl, but you don't see me asking the whole community to pay double the going rate for a turn at the mini-putt so I can work on my tan. Anyways, they charged two bucks for one turn and five for three, and a couple weeks later when Amy Lewis and Dave Saunders had their Stag and Doe, they kept the prices the same thinking that if people were willing to pay that once, they'd be willing to pay it again, even though their wedding was just in Amy's mom's backyard.

BONNIE: They didn't even have a tent! I don't know how she did it—I'd be a basket case!

DEE: Bonnie, relax. Your wedding is in the middle of July, inside a church and in here. It'll be fine.

BONNIE: But what if it's too hot? What if it rains? What if something crazy happens like last night?

DEE: A storm like that comes around once in a blue moon.

BONNIE: That was the first time we've had crazy weather like that out at the farm. Don't get me wrong, it was a good purchase, the barn's in great shape, but the house is a bit...

DEE: Rustic?

BONNIE: It was like *The Wizard of Oz* out there. Brad running around, trying to shut the gates and get the equipment in the shed and me chasing the dog to get her down in the cellar. When it died down and

	we came upstairs, half the willow tree was down across the laneway and the back rack of the hay wagon was all the way over in the beans.
DEE:	Did you check to see if there were any legs sticking out from under your house? That wind was crazy, though. It came out of nowhere. I'd been on nights all week, so I crashed early, but my dad called to wake me up. He just screamed, "Get in your basement, Dee! Get in your basement!" and then the phone went dead.
BONNIE:	You'll always be his little girl.
DEE:	Yeah, but he helped me buy my house, you'd think he'd remember I don't have a basement. OK. What else can I do?
BONNIE:	I guess we can start on these. *(Peeling and cutting carrot sticks.)*
DEE:	Oh! I got you this. *(She pulls an enormous jar of pickles from a reusable grocery bag.)*
BONNIE:	Perfect! How much do I owe you? *(Grabbing her wallet from her purse.)*
DEE:	Put your money away—you're going to need it. This thing cost me like five bucks at Costco in London. I finally had a reason to use my membership. Believe me, when you live alone, it takes a while to get through thirty-six jars of crunchy peanut butter. Oh! But did I tell you who I ran into in the parking lot?
BONNIE:	At Costco? Who?
DEE:	Miss Destination Wedding herself—Becky Walsh—Wasileski—whatever. I asked her if they had tickets to your Stag and Doe yet and she said, "Oh I don't know, maybe Greg was going to get some." So I say, "You guys are planning on coming right? It's this

Saturday. I know how much you love a good Jell-o shooter, Becks!" And she goes, "Well to be honest, I'm not really drinking these days…"

BONNIE: Oh really?

DEE: I don't know for sure if that's what she meant. How could you tell? Ever since grade ten, she dresses like she's trying to hide a pregnancy.

BONNIE: Dee!

DEE: What? Am I wrong? Anyway, I say, "Even if you're not coming, just buy a ticket, Becky." And that's when she goes: "Oh. We don't really do that."

BONNIE: What do you mean?

DEE: Like, "We don't buy tickets to Stag and Does unless we know we're going to go." So I say, "Oh come on Becky, everybody does that." And she says, "Yeah well, Greg and I had a serious talk about our finances and we decided we just don't do that anymore."

BONNIE: Well then.

DEE: I know. So I just look her right in the eye, right in front of the CostCo and say, "Listen up, Becky. I was working the whole weekend of your Stag and Doe and I bought a ticket even though I knew I couldn't come. Hell, Becky, I bought two tickets, knowing full well that even if I could switch shifts"—which I wasn't about to do for her stupid Stag and Doe—"I wasn't going to have a man to take with me." I just gave her twenty bucks and I bought them, because that's what you do. It's not about using the tickets, it's not about actually going to the Stag and Doe, it's about supporting people. "And now, Becky, my best friend—who bought tickets to your overpriced Stag and Doe, and if I remember correctly, even bothered to show up—is getting married. And

| | I still have sixteen tickets in my purse to sell to the stupid thing by Saturday night. So while I'm really happy that I could help bankroll your island getaway, I can't help but wonder if you're planning on raising this little reason you're not drinking to be as ungrateful as you are." |

BONNIE: What did she do?

DEE: Gave me twenty bucks and said they'll try to make it. I get it. Money's tight, you've got to cut back, but where do your priorities lie?

BONNIE: That's the sixty-four thousand dollar question.

DEE: Well, not quite sixty-four thousand... So what did Brad say when you told him?

BONNIE: Oh, you know. Do you know where they keep the kettle in here? *(She starts a hunt.)*

DEE: Bonnie?

BONNIE: We'll need it to make Jell-o.

DEE: Bonnie, when are you planning on telling him?

BONNIE: I don't know! When the time is right! Shouldn't it be down here? *(Looking in cupboards.)*

DEE: When we had my grandparents' fiftieth anniversary, it was over there. So when is the time going to be right?

BONNIE: After tonight. I think they reorganized everything. It was all labelled when I was in 4-H.

DEE: What is he going to do when he finds out?

BONNIE: Why did they move everything? It's been years since I served anything in here. The last time was probably before Brad came along. Must have been a Stag and Doe or something...

DEE: Yeah. That would have been mine.

BONNIE: Oh. Right. Sorry.

DEE: *(Referring to a coffee percolator BONNIE has found.)* Keep that out. We should make coffee and tea tonight too.

BONNIE: We should?

DEE: For the old folks who come at nine and leave by ten. All those people who were friends with your mom.

BONNIE: I guess all them buying tickets is her way of helping out with the wedding. God knows she could never have afforded to pay for it if she was still alive. And my dad...well, I finally tracked down his address but he hasn't even bothered to RSVP.

BRAD enters through the back door.

BRAD: Hey babe. Can I have your credit card?

BONNIE: What for?

BRAD: To pay for the booze.

BONNIE: Why can't you use yours?

DEE: Morning, Bradley.

BRAD: Hey. Can I just have your card, please? I have to go back. Everything's waiting for me at the liquor store.

DEE: *(Getting confirmation on carrot stick sizes, trying to change the subject.)* Is this good?

BONNIE: Yeah. Did you forget your PIN number again?

BRAD: No, I did not forget my PIN number again.

BONNIE: So why can't you use your card?

BRAD: Why do you think? Can I just have yours?

BONNIE: No! What happened?

BRAD: First of all, I was there right at ten when they open, like you told me, and the door was locked. At ten after, that Vandermeyden kid shows up—I don't even know how he works there, he doesn't look like he's old enough to drink. I say to him, "Quite the storm, eh? You have to take the long way in?" and he just glares at me and walks around back.

BONNIE: What does this have to do with your credit card?

BRAD: Another five minutes goes by, I knock on the door, he opens up, I go, "I thought you guys opened at ten." He says, "There's supposed to be two of us here to open the store." And I go, "Well, great. You and me. Two of us here. Brad McKellar. Remember me? I bought those heifers from your dad? I'm here to pick up a case of red, a case of white, four bottles of rye, four bottles of rum, four vodka, two schnapps, two scotch, one tequila, and twenty friggin' two-fours of beer for my Stag and Doe."

DEE: It sounds like a lot when you list it off.

BONNIE: OK, are we getting the booze or aren't we, Brad?

BRAD: So I grab a cart and start getting everything on the list—

BONNIE: Why can't you use your card?

BRAD: And by this time, that old lady who works there—

DEE: Which one?

BRAD: I don't know her name, you guys grew up here, not me. The mean one.

DEE: Oh, Fern.

BRAD: Fern. Holy shit.

DEE: She's my aunt.

BRAD: Oh, sorry.

DEE: No, it's OK. I know.

BRAD: Fern's arrived and comes up to the cash and tells the Vandermeyden kid to go to the back to get the beer. She rings everything through and asks why so much? I say it's for my Stag and Doe. She says, "Who do youse have bartending?" "The volunteer firefighters. I'm one of them. We all did Smart Serve." "You know the hall doesn't have a permit anymore, youse have to get your own." "Yup. Got it, thanks." "Well, to sell youse this amount of alcohol, I'll need to see it." So I run out to the truck to grab it, come back in, show it to her, and then... she friggin' cards me! Can you believe that?

DEE: You know, I'd be flattered.

BRAD: So it's all waiting for me by the door, I just need to pay, OK Bonnie?

BONNIE: What the hell is wrong with your card?

BRAD: The total comes to almost three thousand dollars.

DEE: Whoa! Don't come on an empty stomach, folks! We've got some drinking to do!

BONNIE: Yeah but you called and got your limit raised.

BRAD: No, I called and asked to raise my limit. No dice. Aunt Fern swiped my card five times. She asked if I had another card I wanted to try, but I made the mistake of opening that bill the other day. Then little Vandermeyden comes back and says, "Maybe you should use your debit," because he's still too young to know that most money in the world is imaginary and you won't always have twenty-eight hundred bucks kicking around in your chequing account to buy beer.

BONNIE: You don't have room on your credit card.

BRAD: Yes! That's what I'm saying.

BONNIE: Why not?

BRAD: Why not? Are you kidding me? This wedding is why not. Sitting on that card, I've got the permit for tonight, the marriage license, the photographer deposit, the flowers, the limo. I've got this tux rental even though I own a perfectly good suit. And I'm still trying to pay for that ring! So can I please, please just have your card?

BONNIE: Umm...

BRAD: Is it in your purse? *(He goes to get it.)*

BONNIE: Yeah. I just don't know if...

DEE: *(Putting down the carrot peeler or knife.)* Here we go.

BRAD: You don't know what?

BONNIE: I can't guarantee there's room on that card.

BRAD: What? Your limit is higher than mine, Bonnie.

BONNIE: A bit.

BRAD: I've put all the wedding stuff on my card.

BONNIE: Not all of it.

BRAD: Photographer, DJ, flowers, tux—

BONNIE: Well, sure.

BRAD: What have you put on your card?

BONNIE: The invitations.

BRAD: That was months ago! And I thought you got a good deal online.

BONNIE: I did!

BRAD: So what else is there?

BONNIE: Umm... *(Looking to DEE for back-up.)*

BRAD: What?

DEE: She is going to look beautiful, Bradley.

BRAD: Excuse me?

BONNIE: Remember how I told you I found it? I finally found the one?

BRAD: Huh?

BONNIE: It was definitely the one. Definitely. But it turned out to be a little, tiny bit over budget.

BRAD: What's a little tiny bit?

BONNIE: I just wasn't finding what I was looking for in the price range we talked about.

BRAD: Bonnie...

BONNIE: Just wait till you see it.

BRAD: Bonnie...

BONNIE: I went to so many stores and I couldn't find what I was looking for.

BRAD: Bonnie.

BONNIE: And the wedding day was getting closer and closer and then we walked into that store and it was the one. Wasn't it, Dee? Like, The One.

DEE: It's very pretty.

BONNIE: I mean, I was starting to lose my mind because most brides have their dress months and months in advance. And there I was, two months away with nothing to wear. And alterations take time...

BRAD: How much over budget?

BONNIE: They always say, when you put it on, you'll just know. And some things looked nice, but nothing really spoke to me, you know?

BRAD: Bonnie, how much?

DEE: Oh God.

BRAD: Dee, how much was it?

DEE: You have to understand, Bradley, that Bonnie really feels that this is The One.

BRAD: I understand. I won't get mad, OK?

BONNIE: OK.

BRAD: I just need to know.

BONNIE: Yeah.

BRAD: How much?

BONNIE: I mean, when you think about it, you only get married once, right?

DEE: Maybe.

BRAD: Bonnie, I'm serious. How. Much.

BONNIE: Six thousand dollars.

BRAD: WHAT THE FFF—

BONNIE: You said you wouldn't get mad!

BRAD: My truck didn't cost six thousand dollars!

DEE: Well, that's not surprising…

BRAD: It's a cab and a half, Dee!

BONNIE: I'm sorry, babe.

BRAD: You better be! You obviously have to return it.

BONNIE: I can't.

BRAD: Bonnie, it sounds like you really love this dress, but you have to. It has to go back.

BONNIE: No, Brad. I can't. The wedding is three weeks away. The alterations are done.

BRAD: Tell them to alter it back.

BONNIE: It's a done deal. You have twenty-four hours to change your mind and after that it's final sale.

BRAD: We can't afford it!

BONNIE: Yeah, but after tonight—

BRAD: After tonight, I was planning on making a payment on my million dollar credit card bill. Or my other million dollar credit card bill. Or—call me crazy—paying for the hundreds of thousands of dollars of mortgage we just signed up for. We're not having a Stag and Doe just so we can maybe, possibly pay for one dress!

BONNIE: OK, in the long run, what's six thousand dollars?

BRAD: In the long run, it's—oh, I don't know, let me do the math here—SIX THOUSAND DOLLARS!

BONNIE: Brad—

BRAD: No, wait. In the long run, with interest, it's probably more like twelve thousand dollars.

BONNIE: Can you just sell a couple steers?

BRAD: Or I could sell the whole herd.

DEE: Maybe once you see it—

BRAD: You put her up to this.

DEE: I didn't. I swear.

BRAD: You convinced my fiancée that spending six thousand dollars on a wedding dress was a good idea.

BONNIE: She liked the cheaper one.

BRAD: What?

DEE: I voted for the cheaper one. The one on budget.

BRAD: This might be the only time I ever say this, but why didn't you listen to Dee?

BONNIE: OK! If we sell a lot of Jell-o shooters tonight, then maybe—

BRAD: How many Jell-o shooters are you going to have to sell to raise six thousand dollars?

BONNIE: I don't know. A lot?

DEE: Three thousand. We didn't buy that much Jell-o.

BRAD: Well, if there's no room on our credit cards, there won't be any Jell-o shooters. There won't be any booze and there won't be any Stag and Doe.

DEE: *(Getting her purse.)* There's no need to get dramatic. Give me your keys.

BRAD: What?

DEE: Well, that much booze isn't going to fit in my car, is it?

She grabs BRAD's key from his pocket.

BRAD: What are you doing?

DEE: The last thing this town needs is a dry Stag and Doe.

BONNIE: Dee, you don't have to—

DEE: The wedding party's supposed to host this thing, right? And with your brother in the States, I guess I'm it. I guess you're looking at the wedding party.

BONNIE: I told you, I've been a bridesmaid so many times, I didn't want to put all my girlfriends through that hell.

DEE: Gee, thanks.

BONNIE: You know what I mean. You're the only person I want standing up there with me.

BRAD: Gee, thanks. Do you have room on your credit card?

DEE: No, Bradley, I always keep three Gs in cold hard cash in the trunk of my car in case of an alcohol emergency.

BONNIE: We'll pay you back.

DEE: Damn right you will. It looks like those could use a wipe-down.

> *She tosses one of them a rag or towel to wipe off the games and starts to go.*

BRAD: Careful with my truck!

DEE: Bradley, it's a piece of shit. It's worth less than a dress.

> *She exits. Beat.*

BRAD: What the hell, Bonnie? Six thousand dollars? That's highway robbery.

BONNIE: It's really, really nice.

BRAD: I don't care how nice it is or how much you love it

or how it's The One, it's so much more money than we talked about. It's over four times the amount that we talked about.

BONNIE: Yeah, but—

BRAD: And even then, when we went over how much things were going to cost, I thought we were being pretty generous with the dress budget.

BONNIE: Wedding dresses aren't cheap, Brad.

BRAD: Obviously! So were you ever going to tell me?

BONNIE: Yes, after tonight, when we could pay for it.

BRAD: Do you think we're having this Stag and Doe to pay for a dress you're going to wear one day of your life? That is crazy!

BONNIE: The point of a Stag and Doe is to pay for your wedding.

BRAD: Is that the point?

BONNIE: This happens to everybody, OK? Everybody's wedding costs more than they think it will.

BRAD: Yeah like, "Oh, I didn't know a cake could cost three hundred dollars," not like, "That's correct, Your Honour, my wife's dress is the reason we're filing bankruptcy." What would possess you to spend SIX THOUSAND DOLLARS ON A STUPID DRESS?

BONNIE: IT'S NOT STUPID!

BRAD: Tell that to the bank when we CAN'T MAKE OUR MORTGAGE PAYMENTS!

BONNIE: Don't yell at me!

BRAD: Have you completely lost your friggin' mind? We said we were going to keep this thing small.

BONNIE: It is small.

BRAD: No, small is getting married at London City Hall and having dinner at The Keg.

BONNIE: I told you that was never an option, Brad. We only have one person each in our wedding party, they're paying for their own clothes—

BRAD: The guest list is forty people more than we originally said, every single thing costs twice as much as we budgeted, and now this dress? I was willing to go along with it up to a point, but really? Six thousand dollars, Bonnie? Who the hell do you think we are?

BONNIE: It is my wedding. It is my special day. If everybody else gets to have this, so do I. When my parents got married, my mom made her own dress with fabric my aunt had leftover from making hers. Growing up, when we'd look at the one picture she kept from their wedding, Mom always laughed at how terrible she looked, how cheap she was. She never bought anything new, she never treated herself, and she died never knowing what any of that feels like.

BRAD: You don't know that. And you think your mom really cared about any of that?

BONNIE: The point is, I do. I care. This is my one shot and I'm going to do it right.

BRAD: Who the hell are you, Bonnie?

BONNIE: What do you mean?

MANDY: *(Her voice coming from offstage.)* Hello?

BONNIE: Wait.

MANDY: *(Off, a bit closer.)* Are you guys in here?

BONNIE: Hello?

> *MANDY enters—from the back door or from inside the hall—with an elaborate construction of rollers in her hair.*

MANDY: Bonnie, hey, how's it going?

BONNIE: Mandy? We're kind of in the middle of something—

MANDY: You're Brad, right? I just got a call from Rob, you guys.

BONNIE: Can you just give us a—

MANDY: We have a major issue with today.

BRAD: What's today?

MANDY: Our wedding. He just went out to my mom and dad's place and...you guys...I don't know what we're going to do. *(She starts to cry.)*

BRAD: Oh no, no, no.

MANDY: The whole wedding was supposed to be there. Everything was all set up but then that weather, that wind. After the rehearsal dinner, my mom and dad went to pick up my brother at the airport. He's teaching English in Korea and he flew home for my wedding but they couldn't land the plane until really late because of the storm, so they decided to get a hotel in Toronto and drive back early this morning and they just got home and...I didn't know the wind was that strong, you guys, and... it's gone.

BONNIE: Your parents' house is gone?

MANDY: The house? The house is fine, I'm not talking about the house, it's the tent, you guys. My wedding tent. It's gone.

BONNIE: What do you mean, gone?

MANDY: I mean, like, gone. Apparently most of the floor is still there and some of the poles, but they can't find the tent. It blew off. It blew away. There are tables and chairs and port-o-potties all over the field. My decorations are completely ruined. I spent so much time on them, you guys. *(More tears.)*

BRAD: Here, have a seat. Do you want a glass of water?

MANDY: Do you have any vodka?

BONNIE: We're working on it, Mandy. So what are you doing here?

ROB: *(His voice from off.)* Mandy? Honey? Are you in here?

MANDY: Do not come in here, Robert. I swear to God, you cannot see me today until I am walking down the aisle in my dress.

ROB: *(On the other side of the door.)* I understand that, sweetie, but we need to deal with this, OK?

MANDY: Do not come in here! It's bad luck!

ROB: I think it's a little late for that. I'm coming in, OK?

MANDY: No! You know I'm superstitious!

MANDY hides in the closet as ROB enters, perhaps a bit disheveled from his tent search.

ROB: Mandy sweetie, we need to figure out what we're going to do.

BONNIE: Hey.

ROB: Bonnie?

BRAD: Hey man. Rob? I'm Brad. I recognize you guys from around town, but I guess our paths have never crossed.

ROB: Yeah, probably not. What are you guys doing here?

BONNIE: Getting ready for our Stag and Doe, but—

ROB: Here?

BRAD: Yeah, but we're sort of—

ROB: Tonight?

BRAD: Right, but—

ROB: *(Approaching the closet door.)* Mandy?

MANDY: *(Jousting a broom out of the closet.)* Get out of here!

ROB: Sweetie, did you know Bonnie and Brad are having their Stag and Doe here tonight?

MANDY: Umm…maybe I saw that in the paper.

ROB: When I went to the hairdresser's, Liz told me you ran over here.

MANDY: Uh huh.

ROB: Why did you come here, honey?

MANDY: Turn around, Robert. I'm coming out.

ROB: Mandy, come on…

MANDY: Robert! It is a tradition. I'm serious.

ROB: OK.

He turns and she pops out of the closet.

MANDY: How many people are you guys expecting here tonight?

BONNIE: I know why you're asking, Mandy, and the answer is no.

ROB: Sweetie, what about the church basement?

MANDY:	We would never all fit down there!
BRAD:	How many guests are you having?
MANDY:	Two-fifty for the dinner, and more for the dance.
BRAD:	How big was this tent?
ROB:	Big.
BRAD:	And it just blew away?
ROB:	Quite a storm, eh, my friend? Mandy's dad is checking to see if it's in their horse pasture. I don't think those guys anchored it down right.
BONNIE:	So you need a place to have over three hundred people? Is the arena free?
MANDY:	Liz said they've still got the ice in. Her daughter figure skates year-round.
BONNIE:	What about the high school gym?
MANDY:	Tonight's the prom.
BRAD:	Can you just call and get another tent?
ROB:	It takes a whole day to put up.
BONNIE:	Can you postpone? Rain cheque? Wind cheque?
ROB:	Mandy, can I turn around please?
MANDY:	*(Hiding in the closet again.)* No! Wait! Now.
ROB:	*(Turning.)* Mandy's brother flew in from Korea just for the weekend. My mom's side of the family is all here from out east.
BONNIE:	Do it tomorrow. One of these places has to be free on a Sunday.
ROB:	Mandy's mom thought of that, but the minister has three church services, a baptism, and a funeral tomorrow.

BONNIE:	Well, do the ceremony today and the reception tomorrow.
MANDY:	*(Her voice from in the closet.)* Absolutely not!
BRAD:	So let me get this straight. You're asking—
MANDY:	Robert, turn! *(He does. She reappears.)* We have to have our wedding reception here, you guys. Tonight. It's our only option.
BONNIE:	Sorry, Mandy. No can do.
BRAD:	Bonnie, it's their wedding, maybe we should—
BONNIE:	Nope. We booked this hall a year ago.
MANDY:	Well, I booked my tent a year ago. Shit happens, Bonnie.
BONNIE:	Sure does. You know, that's funny coming from you.
MANDY:	That's in the past! I wish you guys would get over it.
ROB:	Ladies.
BRAD:	What are you talking about?

DEE enters with an LCBO bag containing four big bottles of booze, reading a very long receipt.

DEE:	Look how many Air Miles I got!
BONNIE:	Dee!
ROB:	*(Still facing the other way.)* Dee Dee?
MANDY:	*(Shrinking back into the closet.)* What is she doing here?
DEE:	Cute hair, Mandy! Looks great.
BRAD:	What's going on?

BONNIE: I'll tell you later.

DEE: How's your wedding day going, Robbie?

ROB: *(He turns.)* Fine thanks.

DEE: Sorry to hear about your tent.

ROB: How did you know?

DEE: Liquor Store. Bad news travels fast. So what's up? You want to use the hall?

ROB: Well, I think maybe Mandy was thinking that if it's possible for Bonnie and Brad to find another venue, or reschedule to another night then maybe we could…you know…

MANDY: Robert! Turn!

He obeys.

DEE: Good boy.

MANDY: *(Reappearing.)* You guys have to let us have the hall tonight. You have to.

DEE: They have to?

MANDY: Listen, Dee, I don't know if I've ever had a chance to tell you how sorry I am for what happened.

DEE: I'm pretty sure you could have found a chance in the past—oh, what's it been now?—seven years, Amanda.

MANDY: I know this is bad timing, but I am really sorry and I hope we can be friends.

DEE: Ha!

BRAD: Hold up. You're Robbie?

ROB: Rob.

BRAD:	No, you're the guy who...?
ROB:	Yeah.
BRAD:	*(To DEE.)* And he left you at the altar for...?
DEE:	Yeah.
BRAD:	OK! Well! It was nice having you folks. And I hope everything works out for you today wherever you wind up having your wedding—or not having your wedding—but I'm gonna have to ask you to get the hell out of here.
ROB:	Come on, my friend!
BRAD:	I'm not your friend. I make a point of not being friends with complete assholes.
ROB:	Who are you calling an asshole?
BRAD:	You.
ROB:	Oh yeah?
DEE:	Boys.
MANDY:	We need to use this hall, you guys.
BONNIE:	So do we.
MANDY:	But it's my wedding day.
BONNIE:	It's my Stag and Doe.
MANDY:	A wedding trumps a Stag and Doe.
BONNIE:	Oh, does it? Let me just check my wedding rule book.
MANDY:	I would do it for you, Bonnie.
DEE:	Somehow I have a really hard time believing that.
BONNIE:	The answer is no. It's not going to happen, Amanda.

ROB:	Whoa, whoa, whoa, time out. What are these games doing here?

As ROB takes over, MANDY ducks back into the closet, giving him the freedom to turn.

BRAD:	What do you think?
ROB:	You doing a 50/50 too?
BRAD:	No, a raffle.
ROB:	And you're selling alcohol.
BRAD:	No man, we're having a tea party.
ROB:	You're selling alcohol for profit?
BRAD:	It's a Stag and Doe, yes. What's your point?
ROB:	Mandy, you saw an ad for it in the paper?
MANDY:	This week, yeah.
ROB:	Huh! This place doesn't have a permit anymore.
BRAD:	I know, I got a Special Occasions Permit. It's fine. *(He pulls it out from his pocket.)*
ROB:	Ohhh. But that's a Private Event SOP. That's for invite-only events. You can't advertise.
BRAD:	If you don't advertise, how are people supposed to know about it?
ROB:	And that only permits the sale of alcohol to cover your costs, not make a profit.
BONNIE:	Then what's the point?
ROB:	And unless you have a Municipal Raffle License you're not showing me, you're not permitted to run a lottery or play games of chance. Bam! I can shut this thing down.

BRAD: What? This is the permit they sold me.

DEE: Sorry Robbie, but YOU can shut this thing down? Who died and made you king?

ROB: The AGCO: Alcohol and Gaming Commission of Ontario. I work for them.

MANDY: You used to work for them, Rob. You got laid off.

ROB: My contract ended!

MANDY: You covered a mat leave!

ROB: Not now, OK? I'm trying to save our wedding. I still have Denise's number, I call this in, she comes this afternoon, puts an end to this and every future Stag and Doe in this place. Hall's free. Case closed. We win. Mandy, call the caterer and tell him to come here—we're having ourselves a wedding.

He gets out his cell phone and looks for Denise's number. MANDY does the same, for the caterer.

BRAD: What the hell, man?

BONNIE: Hold up. Did you say caterer?

ROB: Yeah.

BONNIE: Cooking in this kitchen?

MANDY: That's the idea.

BONNIE: Oh, didn't you hear the news? Some guy from the Health Unit made a surprise inspection last week. This kitchen's not up to code.

MANDY: What?

BONNIE: Yeah, something about the lack of separate food prep and dishwashing areas. Lorraine from the United Church Women called me about it because if the town doesn't install a new sink by the time of our wedding, the UCW's going to need to use another certified kitchen to make the meal. The Health Inspector gave this place a red light, so if your caterer cooks in here, I would be forced to call it in.

MANDY: Are you kidding me?

BONNIE: It's a public safety concern, Mandy. We don't want anyone getting sick.

MANDY: Then what is that food doing there?

DEE: We're living on the edge. So…great! You can all throw the book at each other. Wrap the whole thing up in red tape, there's no Stag and Doe, no wedding, and what's the good of that? I do not know why I am even saying this, but is there any way you can share the hall?

MANDY: What do you mean, share?

DEE: I mean, "share". It might be a new concept to you, Mandy. You probably missed that day of Kindergarten.

MANDY: We're not sharing the hall.

DEE: You got a better idea? No calling this Denise person. No calling the Heath Unit. Everybody plays nice.

MANDY: There's no way!

ROB: Mandy, hear her out. What's our schedule for the day?

MANDY: Robert, I have told you a million times!

ROB: Ceremony at three. Cocktails at five. Dinner at six. Speeches at eight. Dance at ten.

DEE: What would you say to a dance at nine?

MANDY: No! Speeches are scheduled between eight and ten.

BRAD: Two hours of speeches?

DEE: Make 'em snappy. At nine o'clock, the official part of your wedding would be over and your guests are welcome to stick around and join the party.

MANDY: I don't think so.

ROB: Mandykins, what's our other option?

DEE: Mandykins?

BONNIE: And as of nine o'clock, we keep all profits from the bar.

MANDY: We're not having a cash bar at my wedding!

DEE: But it wouldn't be your wedding anymore. It would be their Stag and Doe.

BONNIE: And at a Stag and Doe, you buy drinks.

DEE: And raffle tickets.

BONNIE: And play games.

MANDY: Raffle? Games? Cash bar? No way! It's just so trashy!

DEE: Well, so is running off with someone's fiancé on her wedding day, but that didn't stop you before.

ROB: Easy, Dee.

DEE: Oh please, Robbie. I'm the only one who's trying to help you out.

ROB: Mandy honey, can you think of any other place to do it?

MANDY: I don't know! And we'd have exclusive use of the hall until nine o'clock?

BONNIE: We'll just finish this stuff up and get out of here.

MANDY: And you promise your Stag and Doe guests won't do anything embarrassing?

BRAD: We can't promise you a miracle.

ROB: Sweetie, the ceremony's in four hours, what else are we going to do?

DEE: All right? *(Beat. A silent consensus.)* All right! Now let's get that booze inside before it disappears. We've got to get some Jell-o in the fridge—time is money, people! *(She exits.)*

BONNIE: OK. If their guests stay and drink, we'll need more booze.

BRAD: What are you telling me for?

BONNIE: This is our chance to get out of the hole. Can you go get some?

BRAD: *(Gets out his credit card.)* Why don't you go? Try your luck with this.

BONNIE: Brad, I—

BRAD: Oh, my mistake...I thought you needed to pay for your day. *(He exits.)*

BONNIE: Brad! *(She follows him out.)*

MANDY: This is not the wedding I planned. *(More tears. She buries her face in her hands.)*

ROB: Hey hey hey, honey, it's OK. Don't cry. Everything is going to be great. You know why?

> He approaches her—keeping his back to her as he crosses the room.

MANDY: Why?

ROB: Because today is still the happiest day of your life.

Stag and Doe

>*He turns and touches her. Mandy looks up to see Rob looking directly at her.*

MANDY: NOOOOOOOOOOO!!!!!

>*Blackout.*

Scene Two

>*It's now 4:30 that afternoon. There are several boxes and bins around the kitchen, food on the stove, and professional catering supplies on the island. JAY, dressed in half his chef's uniform, is hard at work preparing the food for the wedding. He works away diligently and professionally throughout this scene. As the lights come up, he working while leaving a voicemail.*

JAY: Brody. It's Jay. You're the shift captain. You gotta answer your phone or call me back, dude. You guys were supposed to be here over an hour ago, check your email, there was a venue change. Cocktails start at five and I'm leaving this at...almost four-thirty. Even if you're two minutes away, just call me back.

>*BRAD enters from the back door carrying a couple bags of ice.*

JAY: Oh, thank God.

BRAD: Hey man, I just need to throw this in the freezer.

JAY: There's room in that one. You guys get held up or something?

BRAD: What's that?

JAY: Are you new? My sous chef Tony—you know Tony?

BRAD: No.

JAY: A tree fell on top of his car last night, he cancelled on me last minute. We're down a man in the kitchen, but I'm just glad you guys made it.

BRAD: Oh no, I'm not—

JAY: What was your name again, dude?

BRAD: Brad, but—

JAY: Brad. You get the rest of the ice, two of the other guys can bring in the cake, then start prepping for cocktails. The hall's set up as much as it's going to be. With ten of you, that's three tables each and two on bar. It's a big stretch so let's hustle, OK Brad?

BRAD: I'm not a caterer.

JAY: What?

BRAD: Sorry man, I'm just dropping off some ice for the Stag and Doe.

JAY: The what?

BRAD: The Stag and Doe later tonight.

JAY: Dude, what are you talking about?

BRAD: OK, so Mandy and Rob's tent blew away…

JAY: Yeah, Mandy called and said to come here.

BRAD: When I was buying ice, the girl at the store said the pig farmer on the next concession found the tent in his manure pit. I thought, "Well, that's shitty."

BRAD exits to get more ice. JAY makes another call, hangs up when it goes to voicemail.

JAY: Ughh, come on, dude!

He tries to put the food he's been making in the fridge, but it's full of Jell-o shooters.

JAY: What the—

He takes them out of the fridge and leaves them aside or on top of the fridge—out of view. His phone rings, he answers.

JAY: Hey, where are you guys?... Oh, hey Buddy. *(He checks the caller ID.)* Did you dial the phone by yourself?... Hey, Daddy can't really talk right now, I'm waiting for an important phone call, OK?... That's what you called to tell me? OK cool... OK, I gotta go—love you, Jack... That's where you're supposed to say, "Love you too, Dad." Hello? You there? Nope, OK, bye.

BRAD enters with more ice as JAY hangs up. JAY now moves on to making a sauce at the stove.

BRAD: What's the word?

JAY: Oh, that wasn't them. I hire a crew just to get me through wedding season. The past couple years I've lucked out but this year, they're always late, they sneak food, they steal wine, last weekend I caught this Brody guy in a walk-in freezer with a sixteen-year-old junior bridesmaid.

BRAD: *(Heading to the door again.)* Hard to get good help these days.

JAY: What time's your thing tonight? The Stag and...

BRAD: Doe. Nine.

JAY: This thing, it's just a party, right?

BRAD: Yeah, it's the same as a Jack and Jill...? Where I come from we call it a Buck and Doe, but around here, it's Stag and Doe. That works for me—I like to think of myself as more of a Stag.

JAY: Right. I've never been to one. Not my scene, dude.

BRAD: Well, stick around later. And give us your money. God knows we could use it.

JAY: Blood from a stone, dude. Blood from a stone. *(He receives a text message.)* What does that mean? Hold up—can you stir this?

BRAD: I should get that ice—

> *JAY hands BRAD his spoon and makes a call. BRAD awkwardly stirs the pot.*

JAY: Brody? Hey, thanks for finally picking up, dude. Where are you guys? And what is this text, "Sorry about the cake"?... Whoa whoa whoa dude, slow down... Who took your car? And the van too?... You gotta calm down dude and tell me what's up...

BRAD: Am I doing this right?

JAY: *(He corrects or approves BRAD's stirring while still on the phone.)* Oh, come on. How much was there? Who's was it?... Of course. Do you know how long until you'll get here? Hello? Hello? Brody?

BRAD: Not good?

JAY: Not good.

> *MANDY enters from outside in full bride regalia: dress, hair, make-up, veil, little bridal purse, the whole nine yards.*

MANDY: I knew it. I saw that truck outside. What are you doing here?

JAY: Mandy, hello, congratulations, you look beautiful.

MANDY: Whatever, thank you. You guys don't have the hall until nine o'clock. That's what we agreed on.

BRAD: I'm just dropping off some ice, OK? *(He starts to go.)*

JAY: No, can you keep stirring? *(BRAD does. JAY texts.)* Mandy, hi. I've just run into a bit of a problem.

MANDY: What?

JAY: I'm just trying to get some more info…

MANDY: What do you mean, problem?

ROB enters wearing a tuxedo, corsage, the whole deal.

ROB: Hey sweetie? Everybody's waiting in the limo. We've still got a few more pictures to do.

MANDY: I know that, Robert. I made the photo list.

ROB: Sorry.

JAY: Hey, Rob? Congratulations.

ROB: Great to meet you, my friend.

BRAD: Could I just run out and grab— *(He steps away from the stove.)*

JAY: No! *(BRAD stays.)*

MANDY: What is the problem, Jay?

JAY: My wait staff's not here yet.

MANDY: What? It's four-thirty.

JAY: I know.

MANDY: When were they planning on getting here?

JAY: Well, they were scheduled to arrive at three.

MANDY: And?

JAY: That obviously didn't happen.

MANDY:	Cocktails start at five. People will be here soon.
JAY:	I know.
MANDY:	Are they on their way?
JAY:	Well, they were. *(He is texting again.)*
ROB:	Hey my friend, I don't know if you heard, but we're on a bit of a tight schedule because—
BRAD:	I filled him in.
ROB:	So cocktails kind of have to start on time for dinner to start on time for us to be done by nine.
JAY:	That's not going to happen.
MANDY:	What is going on, Jay?
JAY:	I don't really have the full story—I'm trying to find out. *(Continues texting.)*
BRAD:	My ice is probably melting— *(He steps away to go outside.)*
JAY:	I'm serious. Do not let that burn, dude. *(BRAD stays and stirs.)*
MANDY:	Jay, where are my waiters?
JAY:	One sec. *(Reading a text he has just received.)* From what I can tell, my entire serving staff is in jail.
MANDY:	What?
JAY:	I think if you're caught speeding enough over the limit, the cops can impound your vehicle.
MANDY:	What police station are they at?
JAY:	I don't know, I can ask, but I don't know if it's going to make a difference. *(He texts back.)*
MANDY:	Call Patrick.

ROB: What?

MANDY: Just do what I say, Robert.

ROB: *(Getting out his phone.)* Umm...should I call his cell phone?

MANDY: What do you think, Rob? He's on his way here, he's not at home, is he?

ROB: *(Looking at phone.)* I only have their home number.

MANDY: Oh for the love of God, he's your cousin. Here.

She gives him her cell—probably in a jewel-encrusted case—from her little bridal purse.

JAY: *(To BRAD, switching pots on the stove.)* OK. That one's thick enough. Now do this one.

BRAD: I spent my last twenty bucks on that ice, man.

JAY: Fine! Go! *(BRAD goes—quickly. JAY stirs the new pot.)* Who are you calling?

MANDY: His cousin Patrick. He's on the OPP.

ROB: Hi Patrick? Hey, it's Rob... Yeah. Yeah! Yeah, thanks! OK, so we're at the hall and the caterers aren't here yet because they've been caught speeding, I think.

JAY: I think it's technically street racing.

ROB: Or street racing or whatever.

JAY: And drug possession—

MANDY: WHAT?

JAY: Or something...his phone cut out.

ROB: *(On the phone.)* And drug possession, maybe. *(To JAY.)* Where?

JAY: They're not texting back.

MANDY: I need a drink. *(She finds something to drink and helps herself.)*

ROB: Somewhere between here and London, right?

JAY: Yeah.

MANDY: What is the plan, Jay?

JAY: I just found out a second ago, so—

MANDY: My guests arrive in fifteen minutes.

JAY: I know.

ROB: *(On the phone.)* Yeah, see what you can do, I guess. See you soon. *(He hangs up.)*

MANDY: Is he dealing with it?

ROB: He's calling to check.

    BRAD *re-enters with ice and puts it in the freezer.*

BRAD: Coming through.

MANDY: Jay, listen to me. My wedding has already been severely compromised so I need you to find me some waiters.

JAY: OK. *(Looking through his wallet.)* I have the number of an old restaurant contact. I could see if he's got extra staff, but it's almost an hour's drive. The earliest they'd be—

MANDY: It doesn't matter if it's late, just get them here.

BRAD: No, hold up. We had a deal.

MANDY: This is my wedding, OK? It's my wedding.

BRAD: I can see that.

MANDY: And it's going to take as long as it takes. So you can get out there and stand by the front door and tell all your Stag and Doe people that they can wait for us to finish.

ROB: Amanda...

MANDY: Do not "Amanda" me.

JAY has tried calling to no avail. Now he's back cooking, having left his wallet aside. MANDY fills up her drink as BONNIE and DEE enter from the back. Bonnie has more bags of Stag and Doe supplies—rolls of tickets, etc.—and DEE is carrying a giant Texas Mickey bottle of Canadian Club.

DEE: IS THIS WHERE THE PARTY'S AT?!

MANDY: What are you doing here?

DEE: Oh hi. That is quite the dress.

ROB: Dee.

DEE: So you did it this time, eh Robbie? Good on ya.

MANDY: You gave us exclusive use of the hall—

BONNIE: We're just dropping these off and leaving, OK? *(She starts towards the door.)*

BRAD: Wait. There's a problem with their caterers.

DEE: This just isn't your day, is it?

BRAD: They're not going to be done by nine.

BONNIE: What?

MANDY: Your little party will have to wait.

BONNIE: No, no, no, no, no. What's going on?

JAY: They got held up.

MANDY: By the cops!

JAY: I know this isn't much comfort right now, but I

MANDY: swear to you, the food is going to taste really, really good.

MANDY: It doesn't matter how good it tastes if there's nobody to serve it.

MANDY's phone rings—an obnoxious pop song ring tone—and ROB answers it.

ROB: Patrick, hey, what's the story?... One-twenty in a fifty?

JAY: OK, in the event they don't make it, we can adjust the plan and serve dinner buffet-style.

MANDY: Buffet? Are you kidding me?

BONNIE: Could that happen on time?

JAY: The food is pretty much on schedule, so—

ROB: *(On the phone.)* Really? Does that count as possession or trafficking?

JAY: Oh God.

MANDY: Stop! Wait! Buffet!? Are you joking me right now?

JAY: I could set it up quick and they could come up one table at a time and just serve themselves.

MANDY: This is my wedding, not a birthday party at the Lucky Dragon All-You-Can-Eat Chinese!

ROB: *(Reporting to the room.)* One of them's being detained for questioning on charges of sex with a minor.

JAY: Brody!

MANDY: What kind of caterer are you?

ROB: *(Phone again.)* Wow. Well, thanks for checking... Yeah! We will see you very very soon! *(He hangs up.)*

JAY: OK. Buffet it is.

MANDY: No, no, no! I do not agree to this!

ROB: Sweetie, everybody's on their way.

JAY: The two of you ladies can serve out there and Brad, you can be in here with me.

BONNIE: What?

DEE: No...

MANDY: No way! This is unacceptable.

JAY: I know it is. And I'm sorry. But if we need to be done by nine—

MANDY: These people are not serving dinner at my wedding.

BONNIE: Hey, "these people" are the ones who are letting you have dinner here in the first place.

MANDY: Oh, come on.

BONNIE: And "these people" have the key to the building.

ROB: So?

BONNIE: So "these people" will use it to lock the door until nine if "these people" have to.

MANDY: Bonnie, why are you being such a bitch?

BRAD: Why are you?

ROB: What did you just call her?

BRAD: Nothing.

ROB: That's not what I heard, my friend.

BRAD: Maybe you didn't hear me the first time. We're not friends. *(Gets up in ROB's face.)*

ROB: Oh yeah?

BRAD: Yeah!

DEE: Boys, grow up!

BONNIE: How much are you spending on this wedding, Mandy?

MANDY: None of your business.

BONNIE: Daddy paying for everything? Must be nice. So what's the going rate to save a wedding twice in one day?

BRAD: What are you doing?

BONNIE: Brad and Dee and I will serve at your wedding—for a price.

MANDY: What?!

BRAD: No we won't.

BONNIE: We're in a bit of a cash-flow crisis, remember?

BRAD: I know. But I don't want their money.

BONNIE: Oh so now you're going to be proud? Let me handle this.

DEE: Bonnie, I'm not going out there.

BONNIE: Shit, I'm sorry. *(To JAY.)* Can she stay in here?

JAY: Can you cook?

DEE: I guess so, but—

JAY: Great, then you're my girl.

> *From offstage in the reception hall, the sounds of the first early guests arriving.*

ROB: *(Looking into the hall.)* Mandy honey, there's people here.

MANDY: I can hear, Robert.

ROB: Well, if we're doing the rest of those photos, we should probably go.

MANDY: Are you in charge of this wedding now?

ROB: No, I'm just—

MANDY: I didn't think so.

JAY: Here, chop this really fine and sprinkle it on those, OK?

DEE: OK…

MANDY: No, stop. I do not accept this.

JAY: I know, I understand. I'll cut your bill in half. I'm so sorry for all the trouble.

BONNIE: There you go. And for all our trouble, we'll take the other half.

MANDY: What?

BONNIE: For us to go out there and smile and serve your stupid guests this stupid food—no offence—that only seems fair. Your dad can write me a cheque before the end of the night.

ROB: Honey… *(Peeking through the door; the sound of guests continues to grow.)*

BONNIE: Sounds like they're here. And it sounds like they're hungry.

MANDY: I'm not paying you half my food budget to stand behind a buffet.

BONNIE: OK. That's your choice. See you at nine. *(She starts to exit.)*

DEE: *(To JAY.)* I'd love to stay and chop, but you know how it is…

MANDY: Wait! Stop! I planned everything down to the last detail and now it's half-way through my wedding and you guys are holding me hostage for, like— *(She looks to JAY.)*

JAY: *(Quick math in his head.)* Uhh…six thousand dollars.

BONNIE: Six thousand dollars? Is that all?

MANDY: Is that all? Are you serious?

ROB: Bonnie, come on.

BONNIE: Are you saying you can't afford it?

ROB: Oh, we can afford it.

BRAD: Good for you.

MANDY: It's not as if you'd be paying for it, Rob.

DEE: Busted.

BONNIE: Mandy, I know it seems like a lot of money, but you were spending it anyway.

MANDY: But that was for waiters, and table service, in the tent, and—

BONNIE: One bride to another, I'm just trying to help you out.

MANDY: No you're not! You're just taking advantage of me! And none of this is my fault!

BONNIE: You're right. It's not. I know how much this wedding means to you.

MANDY: You're just saying that.

BONNIE: You've been waiting your whole life for this.

MANDY: Yeah, but it's not—

BONNIE: You've been through so much already.

MANDY: I have.

BONNIE: But today is still your special day.

MANDY: It is.

BONNIE: Your dad will understand.

MANDY: But...he won't want to—

BONNIE: When you think about it, in the long run, what's six thousand dollars?

MANDY: Right.

BONNIE: Payable to me.

MANDY: But I—

BONNIE: Tonight.

MANDY: But—

BONNIE: You know what, Mandy? You deserve it.

MANDY: I do... I do deserve it.

BONNIE: *(Ushering them out the door.)* There we go. Now you two get out there and enjoy yourselves and we'll be out with some food in no time.

ROB: Honey? What just happened?

MANDY: I don't know. Just smile for the camera. *(They exit into the reception hall.)*

JAY: Hey, I'm Jay.

BONNIE: Bonnie.

JAY: That was incredible.

BONNIE: I've been doing some research.

JAY: Any idea where we can find some bartenders?

BRAD: I'm on it. *(He gets out his phone and starts to exit.)*

BONNIE: Hey babe—looks like we're back in the black, eh? You happy now?

BRAD: No, Bonnie. I'm really not. *(He exits.)*

JAY: *(To DEE, with a professional kitchen gadget.)* You ever used one of these before?

DEE: Uh...nope.

JAY: It's easy. Just like this. *(He shows her how, she tries, he tosses BONNIE an apron.)* Here, throw this on.

DEE: Like that?

JAY: *(Reaching around her.)* If you put your hand like this—may I?—it's usually a bit easier.

DEE: Thanks.

JAY: Look at that. You're a natural. *(To BONNIE.)* And you'll be out there, OK? You can head out with these and pass them around. *(Hands her a tray of hors d'oeuvres.)*

BONNIE: What are they?

JAY: Cornish game hen samosas with tamarind dipping sauce, organic sirloin skewers with Roquefort crème fraîche, and five-grain flat breads with goat's milk brie.

BONNIE: Oh shit. Say that again?

JAY: Chicken, beef, crackers and cheese.

BONNIE: Got it. *(She exits.)*

JAY: Sorry, what was your name?

DEE: Dee. Jay?

JAY: Yeah. So if they're the Stag and Doe, what does that make you?

DEE: Oh, I'm just the Maid of Honour. You know how it goes…always the bridesmaid!

JAY: Here. This taste OK to you?

She tastes an hors d'oeuvre. He puts his chef jacket on, loads himself up with a tray, and heads to the door.

DEE: Mmm.

JAY: Here, try it with this. *(She dips it in the sauce.)*

DEE: Mmm!

JAY: It's all right?

DEE: *(Another bite, a full mouth.)* Mmm hmmm.

JAY: I'm going to take that as a yes. So what's the deal, Dee? You too shy to show your face out here?

DEE: Yeah. Something like that.

He exits. DEE's eyes follow him out. She exhales a mysterious little:

DEE: Whew!

Blackout.

End of Act I.

Act II

Scene One

A few minutes to nine that night. The kitchen is a post-dinner-service mess. Throughout the scene, we can hear the sounds of the party coming from the reception hall on the other side of the wall. As the lights come up, JAY is alone on stage cleaning up, and we hear the tinkling of glasses and the voice of the wedding emcee on a microphone.

EMCEE V.O: Oh, you know what that means! Come on, you two. Oh come on, Robbie. Lay one on her like you mean it. *(Beat.)* OK. That'll have to do.

The sound of speeches continues in the background. BONNIE enters with a tray of dirty dishes.

BONNIE: That's all the tables cleared, there's just a few things left on the buffet.

JAY: You're a rockstar.

BONNIE: It sounds like everybody really liked the food.

JAY: Maybe I should ask Mandy for a customer review to put on my website: "He almost ruined my wedding but the chicken was very moist." Did you get something to eat?

BONNIE: No, don't worry about it. You cut your fee in half, you don't have to feed me.

JAY: What? You guys bailed me out. Here, have some of this. *(He plates her some food.)*

BONNIE: OK, thanks.

JAY: It's not like I'm paying those waiters or my sous chef. And I honestly don't make a habit of this, but I could tell Mandy had money the minute we met—and she wasn't exactly a low-maintenance client—so I might have charged her the "premium bridal rate." It'll be fine. *(Gives her the food.)*

BONNIE: Thanks. Hey, where did Dee go?

JAY: Oh, she said she had to run home for a second. I can handle it from here.

BONNIE: *(Getting out her phone, dialing.)* She left? What is she doing? It's almost nine.

JAY: *(Giving her another bit of food or sauce.)* Here, try this.

BONNIE: *(On the phone. Eating.)* Hey Missy. What are you doing?... Oh, good call. Hey—I'm not going to have time to run home before people start arriving, and I should have asked Brad—he went home to do chores, but he's not really talking to me anyway—so can you bring something for me to change into?... I don't know, whatever, something that will fit me. I just don't want to smell like red wine reduction and brown butter beans all night. Just kidding, Jay! This is delicious... Thanks, Dee Dee! See you soon. *(She hangs up.)* OK. I better get those dishes.

JAY: No, eat. So when are you guys getting married?

BONNIE: Three weeks. Or that was the plan, anyway...

MANDY enters from the reception hall, drink in hand.

MANDY: Excuse me. I didn't realize I was paying for your dinner now too.

BONNIE: Oh you didn't? Well, thanks. It's really good.

MANDY: I told my dad about our little deal. He'll do it, but he is not happy.

BONNIE: Everybody got their food, didn't they? If you wanted volunteer servers, you should have called Lorraine at the UCW. *(She exits back to the hall.)*

JAY: How's everything going out there?

MANDY: Fine, whatever. The cake's not out there yet.

JAY: Right.

MANDY: It was supposed to be set up when the guests arrived.

JAY: OK, I'm really sorry—

MANDY: No. No.

JAY: You remember how I don't actually make the cake? You met Andre at one of the tastings, right? The pastry chef? OK, so his kitchen lost power last night in the storm, so the cake wasn't ready by the time I had to leave in my van, so…

MANDY: It's not here.

JAY: It's in the other van.

MANDY: At the police station.

JAY: Yeah.

MANDY: With the drug dealers.

JAY: Uh—

MANDY: And the child molesters.

JAY: No!

MANDY: Perfect! This is just perfect! How are we going to cut the cake if there's no cake?

ROB enters.

ROB: Mandy sweetie, we need to keep things moving, so—

MANDY: There's no cake.

ROB: All right. No cake. No problem.

MANDY: No, it is a problem. *(She drinks.)*

ROB: Do you think maybe you've had enough for now?

MANDY: No, I don't think I've had enough, Rob. Back off.

BONNIE enters.

BONNIE: Hey, the Emcee wants to know if you're cutting the cake or just going straight to the first dance.

ROB: First dance, I guess.

BONNIE: Do you know how long the song is?

ROB: It's, like, the length of a song, Bonnie.

BONNIE: I'm just asking because it's almost nine.

MANDY: It's three minutes, twenty seconds. Just give us a minute, OK?

BONNIE: A minute. I'll let him know. *(She exits.)*

MANDY: Everything is out of order.

ROB: It's not a big deal.

MANDY: Not a big deal? Not a big deal? It's a wedding and there's no wedding cake. There's no tent and no waiters and now there's no cake and we have to do the first dance without cutting the cake and that was not the plan.

ROB: Everything's going to be fine.

MANDY: Stop saying everything is going to be fine! It drives

	me crazy when you do that! I have been planning this wedding for three years, Robert. Three years of being engaged after four years of dating after however many months of waiting around for you to grow a pair—
JAY:	She probably needs my help out there. *(He goes to exit.)*
MANDY:	I'm not paying for that cake!
JAY:	I know. *(He's gone.)*
MANDY:	So don't act like everything is fine, Rob, when this wedding—the culmination of seven years of my life—is falling apart before my eyes.
ROB:	Sweetie, I know you're upset, but let's just go and dance and get it over with, OK?
MANDY:	I don't want to just get it over with! I planned this day down to the last detail. You have no idea how hard I've worked on this wedding, how much time I've spent—
ROB:	You think I don't know? This wedding's been like a full time job for you since the day I proposed.
MANDY:	But you get to act like Mr. Cool Guy because you didn't actually do anything for the wedding.
ROB:	Because you didn't let me! I tried! I asked if I could help and you just shut me out.
MANDY:	Oh please! You didn't want to help!
ROB:	Yes I did! I asked to go to all the tastings with you, I wanted to take you to that wedding show—
MANDY:	Yeah, you wanted to do all the fun stuff. You didn't want to stay up late at night making three hundred wedding favours.
ROB:	Because you told me I was doing it wrong!

MANDY: Because you were! I wouldn't let you do anything for the wedding because you'd just screw it up. Today was way too important to me to let you screw it up too, but I should have just let you at it because God knows it couldn't have turned out much worse than this. *(She pounds back another drink.)*

ROB: Atta girl! Have another one, Mandy! *(He starts to leave through the back door.)*

MANDY: Where are you going?

ROB: I need some air.

MANDY: Is that what you said to Dee when you ditched her?

> *During the last handful of lines, the intro to a slow song plays from inside the hall. BONNIE re-enters with a tray of dishes.*

BONNIE: They're playing your song.

ROB: Just give us a minute.

MANDY: Robert.

ROB: What?

MANDY: Get over here.

> *BRAD enters from the back door. He's changed his clothes to nicer jeans and a button-down shirt.*

Robert. Now.

> *ROB and MANDY exit into the hall.*

EMCEE V.O: There they are, folks! Let's have a round of applause for the happy couple.

> *Off-stage applause and the song continues.*

BONNIE: Hey. That shirt looks nice.

BRAD: Twenty bucks.

BONNIE: Look. Mandy's dad is writing me a cheque. That covers the dress. If enough people stick around and buy drinks, and we sell enough tickets at the door, we stand to make a profit. OK?

BRAD: Where's the raffle tickets?

BONNIE: In one of those bags.

In looking for the rolls of tickets, he finds the trays of Jell-o shooters.

BRAD: What the hell are these doing here?

BONNIE: What? No! Those were in the fridge! They should be set by now!

JAY enters with the last of the dishes.

JAY: Wow. You could cut the tension out there with a knife.

BONNIE: Hey Jay, did you take these out of the fridge?

JAY: Maybe, yeah, why?

BONNIE: They're our Jell-o shooters for tonight.

JAY: Ohhh!

BRAD: Now what will all the desperate drunk girls run their tongues around to look sexy?

BONNIE: Well, there goes that money. *(She goes to throw the trays of shooters in the garbage.)*

JAY: Wait wait wait. I bartended to put myself through cooking school. I specialized in desperate drunk girl cocktails—I might be able to save them.

He gets two pitchers, some leftover wedding

> *champagne, juice, maybe some ice, and gets to work making a new cocktail. DEE enters wearing a hot, skimpy little summer dress. She's carrying a change of clothes (jeans, a top, shoes) for BONNIE.*

DEE: Howdy.

BRAD: Whoa!

BONNIE: Excuse me, Miss? Are you the entertainment? The bachelor party isn't for another couple weeks.

DEE: Shut your face! I'm in scrubs five days a week. I bought this almost a year ago and haven't had anywhere to wear it. Wait, what are you doing?

BONNIE: Trying to save the Jell-o shooters.

DEE: Did we make them wrong? *(She tastes one.)* Ugh! Those are not meant to be enjoyed at room temperature. There are people waiting out front to get in, eh?

BRAD: Already?

DEE: It's the over fifty crowd—they want to show their support but they also want to be home in time to watch the news.

BRAD: Well…here goes nothing.

> *He grabs the Texas Mickey, the rolls of tickets, and exits.*

BONNIE: Are those for me?

DEE: Yeah.

BONNIE: Are they decent?

DEE: Just put them on, woman.

BONNIE: You're a life saver.

> *BONNIE takes the clothes and exits out the door to*

the washroom. The song ends (or it's already over) and as we hear the Emcee, DEE peaks through the door to watch.

EMCEE V.O: OK folks, it's nine o'clock, so we'll be welcoming more folks to the party. And there's Brad McKellar. Hey Brad, I hope that's not all for you!

DEE: Is that Patrick? Oh God, I always hated that guy.

We hear some shuffling of the microphone and MANDY's voice on the mic.

MANDY V.O: Yeah and it's a cash bar now. If this was just my wedding, it would be an open bar, but it's not just my wedding and... *(She starts to break down.)* ...they made me do it...so if you want to go, I understand, just go—

More microphone shuffling and ROB's voice.

ROB V.O: Or stay. Stay and spend all your money and buy raffle tickets and play the games and get pissed and have a good time, my friends. Somebody's got to.

DEE: Whoa. What is going on?

EMCEE V.O: Well there you have it! Have a good time, folks!

MANDY enters from the hall, heading for the back door.

DEE: Are you OK?

MANDY: Like you care. *(She exits.)*

JAY: Weddings, eh?

DEE: You must see a lot of them.

JAY: For what's supposed to be the happiest day of your life, you would not believe the amount of drama.

DEE: Oh, I think I would.

JAY: (*Finishing up the Jell-o cocktail.*) This is either going to be undrinkable or it's going to be the signature cocktail at every wedding I do for the rest of the summer.

ROB enters.

ROB: Did Mandy come in here?

JAY: She went that way.

ROB: Thanks. (*He gets to the door and stops.*) Looking good, Dee Dee.

DEE: Go find your wife, Robbie.

ROB exits.

JAY: (*Offering DEE some of the cocktail.*) Here, try that.

DEE: (*She does.*) Mmmm!

JAY: It's all right?

DEE: How do you do that?

JAY: I have magic powers. Hey, do you want a real drink?

DEE: Sure, that'd be great.

JAY: What's your poison?

DEE: (*Goes to get money out of her purse.*) I'm easy—whatever you're having.

JAY: No, no, no, no, no. I owe you one. Seriously, what do you want?

DEE: A beer?

JAY receives a text message. He checks it and laughs.

What's that?

JAY: Oh sorry, somebody just sent me a picture.

DEE: Oh yeah? Your girlfriend? Wife?

JAY: Ha! No, my mom. It's just my son getting ready for bed.

DEE: Your son?

JAY: Yeah, see?

DEE: Oh my God! Look at those pyjamas!

JAY: Yeah, he's really into ninjas right now.

DEE: Oh my God, he's so cute.

JAY: He's pretty darn cute.

DEE: That's crazy—he looks just like you.

JAY: I know.

DEE: Like, the spitting image.

JAY: Yeah.

DEE: So cute.

JAY: Are you saying I'm cute?

DEE: No, I'm saying he's cute.

JAY: But he looks exactly like me…

DEE: Well, OK, but he's like, what? Six years old?

JAY: He's five. But if he's cute and he looks just like me…

DEE: I think that means that you're cute in the way that a five year old is cute.

JAY: I'll take it. *(He heads for the door.)* Beer, right? Thanks for all your help earlier.

DEE: No problem.

JAY: *(He's at the door.)* And Dee? You look really... You clean up real good.

He exits. DEE sneaks another taste of the cocktail as BONNIE enters with the clothes in her hand.

BONNIE: Hey. Sorry. These don't really fit me.

DEE: Are you calling me fat?

BONNIE: No, I'm calling myself fat. I told myself I was going to lose weight for the wedding, but instead I've been eating my stress about the dress.

DEE: Do you want me to run home and get you something else?

BONNIE: No, it's OK, there are people here already. I need to get out front to work the door. *(Points at DEE's dress.)* Umm...is that thing stretch?

DEE: What, this?

BONNIE: Can I wear that?

DEE: You hussy!

BONNIE: Please? Sorry! Please?

DEE: Fine. But hurry up—Jay's buying me a beer.

BONNIE: Well, well, well!

DEE: No. I don't know. Maybe.

BONNIE: Should I let you keep that on?

DEE: Nah, it did what I needed it to do.

They exit to the washrooms. We hear ROB's voice.

ROB: *(Offstage.)* Mandy?

> MANDY *enters from the back. She spots the Jell-o cocktail on the counter, tries it.*

> *(Off, but closer.)* Amanda?

> *In a moment of panic, MANDY rushes into the closet—taking the pitcher of Jell-o drink and glass with her—leaving her little bridal purse on the counter. ROB enters.*

> Mandy? Where'd you go?

> *JAY enters to get his wallet, which he left aside earlier.*

> Hey my friend, have you seen Mandy?

JAY: Didn't she go that way?

ROB: She's not out there.

JAY: Sorry—don't know. Wasn't Dee in here?

> *BRAD enters from the hall with the big bottle of rye and a roll of raffle tickets.*

ROB: Did you see Mandy out there?

BRAD: Not since her little speech. Hey, you want to buy a raffle ticket...my friend?

ROB: Very funny. *(He exits into the reception hall.)*

BRAD: What about you?

JAY: No thanks. I wouldn't have any use for that.

BRAD: Well, that's perfect! See, some guy named Scott won this thing at a Stag and Doe a couple years ago and the next weekend, he got engaged. But he kept it and raffled it off at his Stag and Doe and my buddy Matt won and now Matt is married to Jenn. Then I won it at their Stag and Doe and I was shopping for an engagement ring two weeks later. Winning

Stag and Doe

this thing is like catching the garter or something. So if you win, just do what we did, keep this thing on the shelf, and then one day when your bride-to-be spends a fortune you don't have, you just take 'er down, dust 'er off, have yourself a raffle, and pray you're not making the biggest mistake of your life!

JAY: *(Reaching into his wallet.)* That is a very convincing pitch.

BRAD: It's two bucks each or three for five.

JAY: *(He pulls out a ten.)* However many that gets me.

BRAD: For you, my man… *(He measures a length of tickets on JAY's arm.)* Here we go. Know your limit. Play within it.

JAY: Cheers.

JAY exits back into the hall. BRAD is about to leave too when MANDY's phone rings—the same ring tone from earlier—in her little purse on the counter. He turns to look at it and the remaining pitcher of Jell-o cocktail catches his eye. He tries the drink and finds it incredibly strong.

BRAD: Hhhhhhhooooo!

He exits back to the hall. MANDY comes out to get her phone, but the door opens or she hears ROB, and she runs back in the closet before she gets to it. ROB enters talking on his phone.

ROB: You can't just disappear like that. Your dad wants to do a father-daughter dance. I told him the wedding was technically over, but he just laid into me about how he paid for everything and he's going to have a dance with his little girl. So call me back, Amanda. When you get this, find me or find your dad.

He hangs up and starts to exit as DEE enters

wearing the change of clothes she brought for BONNIE. She is carrying BONNIE's original clothes in her hand.

ROB: Hey.

DEE: Oh. Hey.

ROB: You changed.

DEE: Yep.

ROB: Did you see Mandy out there?

DEE: No. Runaway bride? Taste of your own medicine?

He starts to exit again and the message alert goes off on MANDY's phone. ROB finds it in her purse.

ROB: Perfect! Umm… I think this is the first time we've been alone since… So I just want to say—

DEE: You know what, Robbie? Forget it.

ROB: I just want you to know that I didn't mean to hurt you.

DEE: Oh, well then…as long as you didn't mean to.

ROB: My timing wasn't ideal, but I think we both know it was probably for the best. You and me, we probably would have been divorced by now. And probably would have had kids and that would have been really messy. We were too young, we were together since high school, you were the only woman I'd ever been with—well, by the time it all went down, I guess Mandy too—but you knew that, right?

DEE: Yeah.

ROB: I just felt all this pressure from you and your family and my family to get married. So I popped the question and once you do that, it's like this rock, you know, like rolling down a hill, like a really big rock, and it just gains momentum and suddenly you're planning a wedding and the rock is picking up speed and the only way to stop it is to step in front of it but I thought if I was just brave and did it, I could stop it from rolling all the way down the hill. So that's what I did, you know?

DEE: You're saying you stepped in front of the rock?

ROB: Yeah, I think so. Yeah.

DEE: OK. No, Robbie. You threw me in front of the rock. You threw me—wearing a wedding gown—in front of this rock while everyone we knew was watching, and you got in Mandy's get-away car and you drove away.

ROB: I didn't think you'd still be mad after all this time.

DEE: Well, that's funny, because I didn't think you'd still be such a moron after all this time, but what are you gonna do? Look, Rob, being left at the altar sucks. I do not recommend it. But I got up and I dusted myself off. And that was hard to do when I was the one stuck taking back the ring, returning the wedding shower gifts, selling the dress, feeling like I owed everybody who came to our Stag and Doe twenty bucks. Being a bridesmaid four times since then. Watching most of my friends have babies already. Nursing your mom when she was in the hospital. Spending New Year's Eve alone thinking maybe this year I'll meet someone. So yeah, you're right, Robbie—you might have saved us from making a huge mistake. But if you're under the impression that you were the one who took the hit, I suggest you take a second and think again.

ROB: I don't think I'm cut out for this.

DEE: For what?

ROB: Marriage.

DEE: Now is a really bad time to figure that out.

ROB: Is this, like, a sign? All of this? The wind storm? The caterers? The cake? Like, is God trying to tell me something?

DEE: Believe it or not, Robbie, I think God has bigger stuff to worry about than your wedding cake.

ROB: You haven't changed. I've missed you, Dee Dee. Can I have a hug?

DEE: Excuse me?

ROB: Can I? Is that weird? Sorry, that's weird. It's just... today's been crazy.

DEE: Oh for the love of God, come here, you big baby.

ROB hugs her, she half-heartedly hugs him back. MANDY opens the closet door a crack to watch, unseen by ROB and DEE.

ROB: I'm sorry, Dee Dee. That's all I meant to say. I'm sorry I threw you in front of the rock.

DEE: OK. There we go.

ROB: I just... I still... I...

He kisses her. A hand-behind-head kiss that she can't immediately escape from. As that happens, JAY enters carrying a beer and a can of coke. MANDY disappears.

JAY: Sorry, there was a line for the bar. *(He sees them.)* Oh! There you go.

The kiss ends; JAY leaves the beer on the counter by the door and exits.

DEE: No, no, no—wait. What the hell, Rob?

ROB: I thought—I thought that you—

DEE: NO!

ROB: I should go.

DEE: Yes. You should.

He goes to the door where BONNIE enters wearing DEE's hot little dress.

BONNIE: Hey, hey, hey! Who wore it better? None of your guests are leaving—you should get out there.

ROB: Yeah. Right. *(He exits.)*

BONNIE: I think word spread around town that our little wedding-crasher Stag and Doe is the place to be. Can you come and work the door for a while?

DEE: Sure.

BONNIE: You OK?

DEE: Yeah. Sorry. Hey—that looks great on you!

BONNIE: If all else fails, maybe I can get married in this. Well, no…if all else fails…

DEE: What? *(BONNIE looks at DEE.)* Oh….hey…he'll get over it.

BONNIE: I don't know! Will he?

DEE: Well, we don't have time to figure that out right now. Come on, girl! Let's go shake our money makers!

They exit. MANDY comes back in from the closet, distraught and drunk, a nearly empty pitcher in her hand. She grabs the other full pitcher and exits through the back door. The lights fade as the sound of the party roars on…

Scene Two

About half an hour later—it's now around ten o'clock. In the transition, most of the remaining mess is cleaned up. JAY is alone on stage packing up the last of this supplies and in the middle of a phone call. The sound of the party in full swing from the hall.

JAY: Wait, Brody, dude...how much was bail? And your dad just paid for it? Yeah, lucky you... No dude, I won't be seeing you next weekend. No... Brody? You're fired.

BRAD enters with a beer.

All of you are fired. And Brody? Grow up, dude. Grow up. *(He hangs up.)*

BRAD: How's it going?

JAY: I have less than a week till my next gig and I have to hire and train a whole new staff.

BRAD: For six thousand bucks a night, I'm always available. Hey, you want to try your luck at the mini putt? Aunt Fern is currently undefeated. Turns out, she was a National Champion in women's golf.

JAY: No thanks, I'm just heading out.

BRAD: You're welcome to stick around, eh?

JAY: Long day.

BRAD: I hear ya.

ROB enters from the back door, where JAY is exiting.

ROB: Still no sign of her, eh?

JAY: Nope. Weird. It seemed to be going so well. *(He exits.)*

BRAD: Hasn't she been gone, like, an hour? Did she just go home?

ROB: As if I didn't think of that. I checked, she's not there. I drove around town looking for her but—

DEE enters, stays by the door.

If she shows up, just keep her in here. I'm just... worried, OK? *(He exits.)*

BRAD: I can't believe you almost married that guy.

DEE: Neither can I.

BONNIE enters.

BONNIE: I'm going to get started on this food. *(She gets things out and starts.)*

DEE: Who's on the door?

BONNIE: Jenn and Matt said they could take a shift. Can you keep an eye on them? Matt's the kind of guy who'd let his friends in for free and everybody's got to pay.

DEE: Sure. Jay's still here, right?

BRAD: Yeah, he's packing up.

DEE: Right. Thanks. *(She exits to the front door.)*

BONNIE: Well! I think we're a hit. Knock wood. They just keep coming.

BRAD: There's twice as many people as we're allowed to have, but all the firefighters are too busy tending bar to shut it down.

BONNIE: Twice as many?

BRAD: Is there enough food for this many people?

BONNIE: Who cares! We've got their money now, eh?

BRAD: Is that what this is about to you?

BONNIE: What are you talking about?

BRAD: Tonight. Making money.

BONNIE: This morning you were freaking out about how we're going to pay for the wedding—

BRAD: These people aren't just here to pay for your dress, Bonnie, they're here to—

BONNIE: What? Help a nice young couple get set for their new life together?

BRAD: I don't know, I guess…

BONNIE: We've lived together for almost three years. It's not like anybody honestly believes we're using this money to buy a toaster. These people are here because this is the only place they have to go out.

BRAD: And if the only point was to make money, we could have just set up a website, asked people to donate fifty bucks, and everybody could have just stayed at home.

BONNIE: The way things are going with these permits, that's not a bad idea.

BRAD: Seriously?!

BONNIE: Look. I know you're upset about the dress, but—

BRAD: This is not about the dress, Bonnie! This is about you.

BONNIE: What about me?

BRAD: I don't know! I thought we were on the same page!

BONNIE: Would you take it easy? After tonight, we can—

BRAD: No, Bonnie! If it's all just about you and your wedding, I just...don't know if...

BONNIE: You don't know what?!

BRAD: I don't know about us.

>*DEE has entered unseen and has heard these last few lines.*

DEE: Hey, a bunch of your mom's friends are heading out before things get any crazier. They want to say good night to you guys.

BONNIE: Umm, yeah, maybe we can cut these in half or something.

DEE: Sure.

>*BRAD exits.*

BONNIE: I don't know, just...just do what you can.

DEE: OK.

>*BONNIE follows BRAD out. JAY enters.*

About what you saw earlier.

JAY: I don't think I want to know.

DEE: No, there's a whole history between me and Rob—

JAY: This happens to me all the time. I meet a girl, we hit it off, and then I tell her I have a kid and—

DEE: Let me explain—

JAY: I get it. It's complicated. *(He exits.)*

DEE: That's not it! Jay?

>*She starts to follow him when MANDY comes bursting through the same door.*

MANDY: Ohhhhh! Look who it is!

DEE: Hey, Rob is worried about you.

MANDY: Ha! That's a good one.

DEE: So stay in here and he'll find you. *(She starts to exit.)*

MANDY: Where do you think you're going?

DEE: To talk to Jay. Just stay here.

MANDY: How many men do you need?

DEE: What?

MANDY: Rob's not enough for you? You gonna steal my caterer too? You wanna fight me for him?

DEE: Who? Jay?

MANDY: No! Rob! You wanna fight me?

DEE: No.

MANDY removes her earrings, veil, et cetera, prepping for a fight.

MANDY: I'm serious. You wanna go?

DEE: Like, "go" or like, "go"?

MANDY: You wanna bring it?

DEE: I don't want to bring anything, Mandy. Can I just—

MANDY: I saw you. You and Rob.

DEE: What?

MANDY: The big boulder going down the hill. *(MANDY gives DEE a little push.)* How he pushed you in front of the stupid rock. *(Again.)*

DEE: Stop it.

MANDY: How much it sucks spending New Years alone. (*Again.*)

DEE: Mandy, you're drunk.

MANDY: I may be drunk, but I know what I saw, Dee! (*She grabs a handful of DEE's hair.*)

DEE: Ow! Let go of me!

MANDY: On my wedding day!

DEE: Let go!

MANDY: You gonna deny it?

DEE: No! But it wasn't my—

BONNIE enters.

Bonnie! Help me!

MANDY: And you!

BONNIE: What? Let go of her!

MANDY: You have ruined my wedding!

MANDY grabs a fistful of BONNIE's hair too.

BONNIE: Ow! No!

JAY enters.

JAY: Whoa, whoa, whoa.

BONNIE: Jay! Help us!

JAY: Break it up.

He tries to break it up. BONNIE becomes free at some point—because of JAY or because MANDY is too busy focussing on DEE.

MANDY: Why is everybody out to get me?

JAY: Mandy, that's enough.

DEE: No, it was Rob who kissed me—

BONNIE: Oh my God!

JAY: *(At the door, calling into the hall.)* Dude! Get in here!

MANDY: What did I ever do to you, Dee?

DEE: What!? What did you ever do to me? Do you want a list?

ROB enters as DEE fights back.

ROB: What is going on?

DEE: She's attacking me!

MANDY: You're attacking ME!

ROB: Come on, break it up.

BONNIE: Stop it!!!

JAY and ROB try to pull the ladies apart. MANDY bites JAY's arm. BRAD enters.

JAY: Ow! Come on!

BRAD: What the hell is going on?

DEE: Help me!

BRAD: Come on, ladies, break it up.

He tries—he might even succeed.

MANDY: Get your hands off of me.

BRAD: Mandy, come on.

ROB: She said get your hands off of her.

> ROB shoves BRAD away from MANDY. In all of this, DEE gets free.

BRAD: What the hell, man?

ROB: Amanda, that's enough.

MANDY: Don't touch me, you asshole!

> She kicks him in the balls.

ROB: Oh God!

BRAD: HA!

ROB: What are you laughing at?

> ROB punches BRAD.

JAY: Dudes! Cool it!

BONNIE: Oh my God! Are you OK?

ROB: No!

BONNIE: I was asking Brad!

BRAD: I'm fine.

MANDY: I am gonna murder you!

> MANDY goes after DEE again. JAY intercepts.

JAY: All right. That's enough. *(He picks MANDY up, carries her over, and puts her on a stool.)* Are you done?

MANDY: No!

JAY: Yes you are.

MANDY: No I'm not!

JAY: You. Are. Done.

ROB: Oh my God, Mandy! That really hurt.

JAY:	Walk it off, dude.
MANDY:	You had it coming.
ROB:	Sweetie, I—
MANDY:	I saw you.
ROB:	What are you talking about?
MANDY:	I saw you kiss her.
BRAD:	What?
ROB:	I, I, I—
MANDY:	I, I, I— WHAT? Is this some sort of sick seven-year cycle?
ROB:	I—
MANDY:	I thought when you left Dee at the altar, that would have been the end of that.
DEE:	It was!
JAY:	What?
ROB:	I uh—
MANDY:	This is our wedding day, Robert. You can't have one foot in and one foot out. This is our life, it's not the Hokey Pokey.
ROB:	Would you just let me talk? Look at you! You've taken this Bridezilla thing to a whole new level. Do you even like me, Amanda? Or did you just want to have a wedding?
MANDY:	I, I, I…
ROB:	There is no "I" in Marriage!
MANDY:	I need a drink.
BRAD:	No you don't.

MANDY: I don't feel so good.

JAY: Do you need to sit down?

MANDY: Yeah. *(ROB tries to help.)* Do not touch me.

JAY: *(Helping her onto a stool.)* Here.

MANDY: Oh God.

BONNIE: Are you going to throw up?

MANDY: No. *(MANDY does her best to feel better.)*

ROB: Are you lying?

MANDY: Yes. *(She starts to head for the washroom. Part way there—)* Nope, not going to make it.

>   *She makes a sharp turn for the sink and throws up. ROB approaches cautiously, holds her hair.*

ROB: I got your hair. *(She throws up some more.)* Just get it out.

MANDY: Can you unhook my dress?

ROB: There you go. You finished?

MANDY: Yeah. *(She stands upright. Beat.)* Nope.

>   *She throws up a little bit more. That last one. Awful.*

ROB: There you go. *(He gets her some paper towel.)* Here. You want a ginger ale?

>   *MANDY nods yes.*

JAY: I got it. *(He exits.)*

ROB: You feel better now?

MANDY: I don't think so... *(She breaks down crying.)*

ROB: Hey, hey, hey...

MANDY: I thought if it was big enough and perfect enough, everything would be better. My dad might get off your back for once, I might finally feel like the princess everybody always said I was. You might get your shit together. I thought if we had the perfect wedding, I would— I should have known.

She exits to the washroom. JAY re-enters with the ginger ale. ROB stands frozen.

JAY: Here we go.

DEE: Robbie...go to her.

ROB takes the ginger ale and exits. Beat.

JAY: Everybody all right?

DEE: Yeah. How is it out there?

JAY: Uhhh...some girl named Becky Wasi-something said you promised there'd be Jell-o shots.

DEE: Oh my God, they came?

DEE and JAY look in the sink.

DEE & JAY: Umm...

BONNIE: I'll go tell her we don't have any. Can you— *(Meaning the food.)*

DEE: Yeah.

BONNIE: And can you— *(The front.)*

BRAD: Everybody pays. I know.

BONNIE exits to the hall, BRAD to the front. DEE starts to work on the lunch; she tries to open the giant jar of Costco pickles. JAY has rinsed the sink out a bit and now continues to pack up.

JAY: I think I owe you an apology.

DEE: It's all good. Me and Rob? Ancient history.

JAY: You need a hand with that thing?

DEE: I think I got it.

> *JAY's phone rings. She continues trying to open it throughout the next few lines until she gives up and moves on to another task.*

JAY: Sorry. You mind?

DEE: No, go ahead.

JAY: (*Answering his phone.*) Hey Mom, everything OK?... Yeah sure... Hey Buddy, why aren't you in bed?... You had a bad dream? What happened?... Yeah? And then what?... And you were all alone, eh? That sounds pretty scary. Well, you know what? You've got your ninja pyjamas on, right? So if those guys come back in your dream, I bet you can use your ninja powers to fight them off... Yeah. We were all just practising our ninja moves. Do you think you can go back to sleep?... OK, I'll pick you up at Grandma's in the morning. And Jack? I love you... You do? Thanks... Oh, hey mom... Yeah, see you in the morning. Night.

> *He hangs up. Takes a second. The music has changed somewhere in here; it's now a slow song. JAY opens the pickles.*

DEE: I loosened it.

JAY: Yep.

DEE: I mean...thank you. Oh, I love this song.

JAY: Oh yeah? I don't think I know it.

DEE: So do you just have him on weekends, or...?

JAY: Nope, full time.

DEE: Wow. Where's his mom?

JAY: Last I talked to her, she was in BC. She was from a very different time in my life, you know? But that little dude is the best thing that ever happened to me.

DEE: Do you want to go dance?

JAY: What?

DEE: Do you want to go and dance? Out there.

JAY: Oh, I'm not much of a dancer.

DEE: Sorry. Never mind. I just like this song. Never mind.

JAY: No, no, no, I mean—

DEE: No, I was just kidding. Don't worry about it.

JAY: Do people still slow dance?

DEE: I know, eh?

JAY: I'd probably just dance like a teenage boy. Here. Is it like this?

He puts his hands on her hips. He dances like a teenage boy.

DEE: Yeah, that's OK.

JAY: Sorry, I look like an idiot. Sorry.

She breaks away, flicks off a couple lights, comes back.

DEE: There. Better?

JAY: OK.

DEE: Now give me this hand. And then that hand can go

	here. There. More like that. You're allowed to stand closer, we're not going to get in trouble.
JAY:	I told you I wasn't a dancer.
DEE:	You are. This is all it is. You got this thing.
	They dance.
JAY:	This is nice. Why don't people slow dance anymore?
DEE:	I don't know.
	BRAD enters. The dancing breaks up.
BRAD:	Hey. Sorry. Hey.
DEE:	Hey.
JAY:	Hey.
	DEE flicks the lights back on.
BRAD:	Sorry. How's this stuff coming along?
DEE:	Fine. No one can say you didn't have pickles.
JAY:	I should let you guys do that. I need to get this stuff in the van.
DEE:	Just…find me before you go, eh?
JAY:	Deal.
	JAY exits. BONNIE enters from the hall.
DEE:	How's Becky?
BONNIE:	She wants a word with you.
	DEE starts to exit. MANDY enters, maybe wearing ROB's tuxedo jacket over her dress.
DEE:	She's alive! *(She exits.)*

MANDY: I just need my purse.

ROB enters with the cheque, which he hands to BONNIE.

ROB: Um. Mandy's dad gave me this.

BONNIE: Right.

ROB: You ready to head out?

MANDY: Yeah.

MANDY and ROB are almost out the door.

BONNIE: Hey, you guys? *(ROB and MANDY stop.)* Just... congratulations.

ROB: Right.

MANDY: Yeah. Thanks.

ROB and MANDY exit. Somehow, we can see there is hope for them. BONNIE and BRAD look at each other. An uncomfortable silence. BRAD starts to exit.

BONNIE: I never should have gone to Foodland.

BRAD: *(He stops, turns.)* What?

BONNIE: The day after we got engaged. I was in the check-out line and I picked up one of those wedding magazines. And OK, I admit it! I had bought them before. I bought them before we were engaged, I bought them before I even knew you.

BRAD: What? Why?

BONNIE: I don't know, Brad! I don't know! You buy Playboy, I buy Modern Bride. But that day, I grabbed one and the girl at the cash—you know Taylor who I used to babysit—looked at me and said, "Oh my God, Bonnie! Are you getting married?" And I said, "Yeah! I am!" And she wanted to see the ring and know all about how you proposed and asked if we'd picked a date and what kind of dress I wanted and all of a sudden, it wasn't just a fantasy. I was a bride. And I started watching those dress shows on TV and I set up a Pinterest page and I started reading wedding blogs and I told myself it was just to get ideas, but before I knew it, I was standing in front of a three-way mirror thinking, "If I love him and he loves me, then yes, what's six thousand dollars?" Because the minute you have a ring on your finger, that's all anybody wants to talk to you about. And the minute you say the word "wedding", everything magically doubles in price. And I swore, I always swore I wouldn't fall for all that crap, but I did. And instead of facing the fact that my mom couldn't come dress shopping with me and my dad refuses to be there to walk me down the aisle, it was a hell of lot more fun pretending I was Kate planning my wedding to Will.

BRAD: Who?

BONNIE: Never mind. So there. I screwed up. Big time.

BRAD: Yeah. So.

BONNIE: So. *(She looks at the cheque and overcome with emotion, she rips it up.)*

BRAD: What are you doing?

BONNIE: The florist said we can get our money back up to a week before.

BRAD: What?

BONNIE: I can cancel the DJ—we'll just lose the deposit.

BRAD: Uhh…

BONNIE: You can get a refund on the tux rental.

BRAD: I... OK. *(Heartbroken, he starts to leave.)*

BONNIE: Do you... Do you still just want to wear your suit?

BRAD: *(He stops, turns.)* Yes...

BONNIE: On Monday, I'll call and cancel the limo.

BRAD: OK. But how will we get around?

BONNIE: There's four of us in the wedding party, Brad. We have a cab and a half. In the long run, none of that stuff matters, does it? I don't know... We'll figure it out.

BRAD: Yeah, babe. We'll figure it out.

BONNIE: Oh my God. You are going to cry at the wedding!

BRAD: Only when I see that friggin' dress.

BONNIE smacks him. They kiss. DEE enters.

DEE: Get a room!

BONNIE: How's it going out there?

DEE: You can't even move! Becky's not pregnant—she's into the tequila and playing roulette trying to win her twenty bucks back, Mandy's brother is teaching everybody the latest Korean dance craze, and that Vandermeyden kid from the liquor store just grabbed my ass.

BONNIE: Do they need something to soak up the booze?

DEE: Can't hurt. Everybody's asking where you guys are.

BRAD: Are these ready to go out?

BONNIE: Yep, I'm right behind you.

BRAD exits with food, BONNIE picks up a tray.

BONNIE: Hey—do you still have the name of that consignment store where you sold your wedding dress?

DEE: I could look it up, yeah. Why?

BONNIE: I'm going to need it in about a month.

BONNIE exits to the hall. JAY enters.

JAY: I was just thinking... I don't know if you'd be into it, and it's totally OK if you're not—but I haven't been to a movie that's not, like, a kid's movie in a really long time—I don't really have anyone to go with—I don't even know what movies are playing. But if you're free or whatever, maybe we could go see, like, a grown-up movie.

DEE: That sounds good.

JAY: And if you want to come over for dinner before...

DEE: I would really like that.

BRAD V.O.: Hey everybody, we're going to do this raffle thing now.

JAY: Where did I put those?

BRAD V.O.: HEY! OK! For this big old bottle of the finest Canadian Club. Hey babe...reach in here and get a number.

JAY finds the long strip of tickets in his pocket or wallet. These next lines can almost overlap:

BONNIE V.O.: OK the winning number is 5 8 3...

JAY: OK...

BONNIE V.O.: ...6...

DEE: *(Helping him check.)* Yeah, come on.

BONNIE V.O.: ...4...2!

DEE: Yeah!

JAY: Yeah?

DEE: YEAH!

BRAD V.O.: Do we have a winner?

DEE runs to the door and shouts into the hall.

DEE: We have a winner! *(To JAY.)* We have a winner.

They look at each other as the lights go to black...

The End.

Bed and Breakfast

Climax → vandalism of house, don't know if they'll stay

turning point ↗ realizing the townspeople are nice + accept them
(+ finding out about his parents)
(+ Ray saying they hated Toronto)

resolution
↓
they stay + open the B+B

rising action ↗ arguing over PDA and the altercation with the truck driver

complication
↳ they've left the house + decide if they will stay since it's in a rural town

exposition
↳ getting the call + meeting everyone at the funeral

O = round character
— = flat character
X = N/A

Characters

Bed and Breakfast is performed by two actors. This is Brett and Drew's story and in order to tell it, they take on all the other roles. To keep things straight (so to speak) I've indicated the first initial of the person who's speaking along with the character he's taking on (ie. D/DOUG or B/ALISON). Here's the complete list of characters, listed under the one who plays them:

- O BRETT, an interior designer, thirties
- — Lynda, his mom, sixties
- — Steve, his older brother, about forty
- — Jeffrey, a barista with attitude
- — Ray, a real estate agent and friend
- — Alison, a cafe owner, thirties
- O Dustin, Carrie's son, sixteen
- — Little Girl, freaking out, six
- — Sharon, married to Chuck, British
- — Sylvia, right-wing, about seventy
- X A Voice, male, older

- O DREW, a concierge at an upscale hotel, thirties
- X Reverend, the voice of a Minister
- — Martin, Brett's dad, sixties
- — Cody, Brett's nephew, Steve's son, eighteen
- — Carrie, a real estate agent and friend
- O Doug, a contractor, late fifties
- — Harold, a neighbour, eighty-one
- O Chris, married to Alison, Irish, about forty
- — Chuck, married to Sharon, British
- — Travis, just married to Alexa
- — Alexa, just married to Travis

Setting

The play is set in various locations in Toronto and a small town a few hours' drive from the city. Because of the speed at which things move, one set should represent all of the locations in the play. Whatever scenic elements there are might suggest the architecture of the house or give us a glimpse into the modern elegance Brett creates for the B & B.

Props and Costumes

There is likely no time for real props, but everything can appear out of—and disappear into—thin air through the use of mime. There is also no time for costumes pieces to differentiate characters; that's all done through the power of acting. There are opportunities, however, for Brett and Drew to change their clothes, showing us how they transform over the course of the play.

Shifts

The changes between locations, times, and characters should be seamless, instantaneous, and most of all, crystal clear. I've used the word Shift to signal a new scene, likely with the help of lights and sound. Think of Shift as driving standard: you change gears, but you keep moving forward...

→ 4th wall breaks

→ foreshadowing the family secret

Production History

Bed and Breakfast premiered at the Thousand Islands Playhouse in the summer of 2015 with the following cast:

BRETT .... Andrew Kushnir
DREW .... Paul Dunn

Directed by Ashlie Corcoran
Set and Costume Design by Dana Osborne
Lighting Design by Rebecca Picherack
Sound Design by John Gzowski
Stage Manager: Michael Barrs
Assistant Director: Krista Colosimo

Act I

In the dark, a phone rings...a cell phone. Fumbling. A lamp goes on. Two men in bed.

BRETT: Hello?...Yeah, hi, it's me.

DREW: What time is it?

BRETT: No, it's OK, I was awake.

DREW: No he wasn't! He's lying!

BRETT: Shhh! No, it's fine.

DREW: If it's work, tell them they can't call this early.

BRETT: No, Dad, it's fine. What's up?

Now another cell phone rings—a different ringtone. DREW turns on his bedside lamp.

DREW: What. In. The. Hello?

BRETT: I am sitting down.

DREW: Ray, do you know what time it is?

BRETT: Is everything OK?

DREW: Yeah well, it didn't go to voicemail because unlike you, I actually answer my phone, so here I am.

BRETT: Oh my God.

DREW: What can possibly be so urgent that you're calling at six a.m. on a Sunday?

BRETT: When?

DREW: What!?

BRETT: Oh my God.

DREW: Oh my God!

BRETT: Did they say if it was uh—

DREW: *(To BRETT.)* Is everything OK?

BRETT: *(Doesn't answer or waves him off.)* Did they say where?

DREW: Wait wait wait—it went for how much?

BRETT: Do we know what happened?

DREW: *(To BRETT.)* What's wrong?

BRETT: *(He looks at DREW. Into phone.)* Yeah, I'm here. I'm just uh—

DREW: Ray, I have to go.

BRETT: Yeah, Drew's right here, we're at home.

DREW: It doesn't matter, I'll talk to you later.

BRETT: Should I come to your place?

DREW: I don't care, Ray, I have to go.

BRETT: Do you want me to call Steve?

DREW: I'm hanging up.

BRETT: You called him already?

DREW: Bye.

BRETT: OK.

DREW: What is going on?

BRETT: Bye. *(They look at each other. Beat.)* My uh…Aunt Maggie was in a car accident last night.

DREW: Oh my God.

BRETT: It looks like the other car ran a stop sign so—

DREW: Is she OK?

BRETT: No. She's dead.

DREW: Oh sweetie, I am so—

BRETT: That was Ray?

DREW: Yeah.

BRETT: Did we lose that house?

DREW: Yeah.

BRETT: Shit.

DREW: Brett…are you OK?

BRETT: I don't think so.

Shift. To us: transitional speech (4th wall)

DREW: When someone asks, "How did you guys end up living here?" I would probably say that that was the beginning. Six a.m. Fifteen floors up, back in Toronto. Exactly one year ago—to the day.

BRETT: But the full story starts long before that.

DREW: Well, sure, but you never have the full story when you're in the middle of it.

BRETT: Especially when there is so much hidden away. A few days later. In my Aunt Maggie's House. Here.

Shift. DREW *reads from the newspaper. They get dressed for the funeral.*

DREW: "It is with great sadness we announce that Margaret 'Maggie' Brooks died suddenly in the early hours of August 31. She was fifty-four years old. An active and beloved member of the community, she will be greatly missed by many. Maggie is survived by her brother Martin (brackets) Lynda of Oshawa. Loving aunt to Steven (brackets) Shannon and their son Cody also of Oshawa and Brett of Toronto." No Brett (brackets) Drew?

BRETT: I noticed that.

DREW: How come?

BRETT: I don't know, I didn't write it.

DREW: Who did?

BRETT: Probably my dad?

DREW's cell phone rings. He answers.

DREW: Hello? No...no, I took the day off, Wesley. I'm out of town... No, I'm a couple of hours out of town, I'm going to a funeral, I told you about this, you said I had so much overtime built up— It's my partner's aunt's funeral, but I don't really see why that matters, Wes. Britney should be able to handle it by now. Wes, I can't— We're just getting ready to— OK. See you tomorrow.

BRETT: What's he want?

DREW: He's freaking out because the film festival starts this week and the hotel's completely booked up.

BRETT: Not your problem.

DREW: If I want this promotion, it kind of is.

BRETT: *(Beat.)* It is so weird to be in this house knowing she's gone.

DREW: *(Picking a tie.)* This one or this one? *(BRETT points to the more conservative one. Beat.)* I thought eight years together might earn us a Brett (brackets) Drew.

BRETT: It's not personal, it's my family, you know they're very—

DREW: Closety?

BRETT: I was going to say private.

DREW: Shannon gets her name in there and they're divorced.

BRETT: Separated.

DREW: She moved to the Yukon.

BRETT: It's a small town paper. My Dad probably didn't want people reading the obituary and only talking about the "Brett (brackets) Drew" part. Today's not really about that, OK?

Shift. BRETT gives the eulogy. DREW, facing upstage, becomes the REVEREND.

BRETT: Thank you all for coming. The summer I was nine, my Aunt Maggie asked if I'd like to come out here and stay with her for a week.

D/REVEREND: Earth to earth.

BRETT: That week turned into the whole month of August and every summer after that till my final year of university.

D/REVEREND: Ashes to ashes.

BRETT: I know how much this community meant to her. And in a way, I feel like I grew up here.

D/REVEREND: Dust to dust.

BRETT: It was here that she taught me how to cook…which explains why I can't follow a recipe…

D/REVEREND: Give us this day our daily bread.

BRETT: She taught me to work hard…I know many of you ladies here will miss Maggie doing your hair—her skill, her style, and her strict "no gossip" policy in the chair.

D/REVEREND: And forgive us our trespasses.

BRETT: She taught me that even if life doesn't go according to plan, you can always make the best of it by making things better, richer, weirder for other people.

D/REVEREND: As we forgive those that trespass against us.

BRETT: I have no way of knowing what I'd be like if I didn't have that time with her.

D/REVEREND: The power and the glory.

BRETT: But I do know that I would be different.

D/REVEREND: Forever and ever.

BRETT: I uh…sorry…I will miss her.

Shift. To us:

DREW: After the burial, hundreds of people pack into the church basement.

BRETT: So many familiar faces from my summers here.

DREW: Ladies serve little sandwiches, squares, coffee, tea.

BRETT: I can't stop thinking: I never told her how much that time meant to me.

DREW: And I can't stop thinking: if I died tomorrow, would anyone care enough to make Nanaimo bars? Among the crowd is Brett's Mom, Lynda…

B/LYNDA: So, Drew, how are things going in the hotel/hospitality industry?

DREW:	The same. Busy. Thanks, Lynda.
B/LYNDA:	Did you get something to eat?
DREW:	Yes, thanks. All of this reminds me so much of home.
B/LYNDA:	Do you get back there much? *(Spotting the REVEREND, unseen to us.)* Oh, Reverend! Lovely service. I don't suppose you met Drew. This is Drew. Our son Brett's…friend.
DREW:	*(To us.)* Brett's brother, Steve…
B/STEVE:	Nice speech, ya friggin' cry-baby. ★ homophobia
DREW:	And Steve's son, Cody… *(He becomes CODY, filling a plate with sandwiches.)*
B/STEVE:	So how's life downtown, boys? How's the condo? I swear to God, I don't know how you two don't kill each other living in that shoebox. I'd go friggin' nuts. Cody, for Christ's sake! How many of those sandwiches are you going to eat?
D/CODY:	I dunno.
B/STEVE:	You'd think I don't feed this kid. Jesus H. Christ! Shit, sorry Reverend. *(STEVE goes. BRETT is back to himself.)*
BRETT:	So Cody, how's Grade Twelve going?
D/CODY:	I dunno…it just started yesterday, Uncle Brett.
BRETT:	Right. Any thoughts on university?
D/CODY:	I dunno…I thought I might go live with mom, but she— I dunno.
BRETT:	How's your girlfriend?
D/CODY:	I dunno…OK I guess.
BRETT:	Great. And when does hockey start up again?

D/CODY: I dunno…I'm not playing this year. Dad's pissed, but I dunno, I'm not really a hockey guy any more, you know what I mean?

BRETT: Yes, Cody. Yes I do. *(To us.)* And my Dad, Martin…

D/MARTIN: What do you mean you haven't found a house yet?

BRETT: We're still working on it, Dad.

D/MARTIN: What seems to be the hold up?

BRETT: We keep making offers at the very top of our budget and we keep getting out-bid.

D/MARTIN: How many houses have you offered on?

BRETT: Seven. We really thought we had a chance with this last one, but—

D/MARTIN: You know what your problem is?

BRETT: We're not millionaires?

D/MARTIN: No son, your problem is you're too picky. Look, I wanted to wait till we were alone, but you might as well know now. Maggie left you the house.

BRETT: What?

D/MARTIN: I'll need to drive back out here and meet with the lawyer later this week, but yes…she did. So. There you go. *(MARTIN walks away.)*

BRETT: I, uh— I—

D/CARRIE: *(Approaching.)* Oh my God, Brett?

BRETT: Oh. Hello.

D/CARRIE: Oh my God, you look amazing!

BRETT: Oh. Thank you.

D/CARRIE: Seriously. Amazing. Time has been good to you. I mean, you didn't get fat. Unlike some people I could mention. *(She means herself.)* Oh my God, I'm so sorry about your aunt.

BRETT: Thank you.

D/CARRIE: She was the best. So active in the community. Such a character, eh? And so sudden.

BRETT: Yeah.

D/CARRIE: Oh my God, Brett, I saw you on TV! Giving decorating advice.

BRETT: Design, yeah.

D/CARRIE: That must be fun, eh? Mr. Big Shot!

BRETT: Oh, the design firm I work for likes me to do those things. Hey, Drew... The TV thing doesn't pay, but it's good promotion for the company. Have you met Drew?

D/CARRIE: Oh my God, no! It is so nice to meet you, Drew.

DREW: Nice to meet you too. Sorry, you are...

D/CARRIE: Oh, I'm an old friend of this guy from back in the day. Well done snagging this one for a husband.

BRETT: Oh, we're not married. Yet.

D/CARRIE: Well, you should be! Look at you! I mean, gay guys, right? You always look good. Oh, that's a stereotype. But a nice one. I mean, look at these suits. You probably don't dress like this all the time—

BRETT: Not really, no.

D/CARRIE: But you look good. Oh my God, Brett, I'm so happy for you! And so sad. So sad for you too. But it's great to see you. Nice to meet you, Drew. Gotta run. Work, work, work. But be in touch, OK? *(And she's off...)*

BRETT: Definitely. Will do.

DREW: Who was that?

BRETT: I have no idea! That's why I called you over here.

DREW: I tried!

BRETT: Maggie left me the house.

DREW: What?

BRETT: My dad just told me. I think he's upset. I assumed she'd leave it to him, he probably did too, he did grow up in it, not that any of us expected her to die first, but—

DREW: Whoa whoa whoa, what does this mean?

BRETT: It means we own a house.

DREW: Here.

BRETT: Yeah...

Shift. Sounds of a gas station.

BRETT: Doug? It's Brett. Brett Brooks.

D/DOUG: Oh yeah.

BRETT: How are you doing, Doug?

D/DOUG: Business ain't worth a shit.

BRETT: Sorry to hear that. I didn't see you at the funeral.

D/DOUG: No. Shoulda went, but I uh— Brenda died in February. Breast cancer. Son of a bitch.

BRETT: Oh Doug, I'm so sorry. Maggie would understand.

DREW: (*Entering the scene.*) Hey sweetie, their debit is down, do you have any cash?

BRETT: Oh, hey, yeah. Uhh...this is Doug.

DREW: Doug, hi, nice to meet you. I'm Drew.

BRETT: Drew's my...umm...

DREW: Partner.

BRETT: Partner...sorry. I worked for Doug the last couple summers I spent out here.

DREW: Oh, Doug? Oh! Doug. Right. Brett's talked about you.

BRETT: All good things. I learned a lot about construction, the different trades, all that. I still use a lot of that for work.

D/DOUG: Oh yeah. You a contractor?

BRETT: Um, I work with contractors. More on the design end of things. Interior...design.

D/DOUG: Oh yeah. Well. Sorry about Maggie. (*He goes.*)

BRETT: (*Calling after him.*) Good to see you!

DREW: (*To us.*) Back in Toronto!

Shift. Sounds of the city.

B/JEFFREY: Next!

DREW: Morning, Jeffrey. Just the usual, please.

B/JEFFREY: Which is...?

DREW: Grande latte.

B/JEFFREY: Your name?

DREW: Drew. (*Beat. A blank stare from JEFFREY.*) D-R-E-W.

B/JEFFREY: Four eighty-nine.

DREW: Yeah.

B/JEFFREY: Swipe towards me.

DREW: Uh-huh.

B/JEFFREY: Your beverage will be at the end.

DREW: Thanks, Jeffrey. I know.

> *Shift. A split scene. BRETT is on TV. DREW is at work.*

BRETT: And our next question comes from Wanda in Sudbury. Wanda is asking about painting some of the wood in her living room. Let's take a look.

DREW: *(Answering a ringing phone.)* Good morning, front desk, this is Drew.

BRETT: Wow, Wanda, that's a lot of wood.

DREW: Oh hey Wesley, yes, I sorted out the situation in 1610. I gave them a gift certificate to the spa and that seemed to calm them down.

BRETT: I can't really tell from these photos, they're all pretty dark.

DREW: *(Answering a ringing phone.)* Front desk, Drew speaking.

BRETT: The room would look a lot brighter if you painted out some of that panelling.

DREW: I'm so sorry for this confusion, ma'am, I left a note about your late check-out for my colleague Britney, but I guess she didn't see it.

BRETT: I think a nice off-white. Maybe Benjamin Moore White Dove OC-17.

DREW: *(To hotel guests.)* Hello, welcome! Mr. Pitt, Ms. Jolie, let me show you to your room.

BRETT: That should brighten things up for you Wanda and really allow that collection of taxidermy to pop off the walls.

The front desk phone rings again. DREW answers. Shift.

DREW: Good evening, front desk.

B/RAY: Girl, we need to talk.

DREW: *(A quick time-out. To BRETT.)* OK, no, that is not what Ray sounds like and you know it.

BRETT: This is exactly what Ray sounds like. *(Back to the scene and RAY.)* Girl, what is all this Brett tells me about his aunt's house?

DREW: Ray, what are you doing calling me at work?

B/RAY: You weren't answering your cell. What are you still doing at work at this hour? Girl, you need a new job.

DREW: No, I need a promotion. And what? You're not still working?

B/RAY: Oh, I'm not allowed to make a personal call now? I am calling not only as your real estate agent, but as one of your dearest friends.

DREW: One of my oldest friends.

B/RAY: Bitch. So what is the story, girl? Isn't that place three hours out of town?

DREW: In bad traffic. We're not moving there, Ray, we're just going back next week to get it ready to put on the market. We'll let you know when it's ready to list. Then when it sells, we'll use that money to get

	a house here. Sorry, Ray, I have to go. I'll talk to you next week when we get back.
B/RAY:	Don't work too hard, girl. And whatever you do, do not fall in love with that place.
BRETT:	*(To us.)* The next week. That place.

Shift. BRETT is sitting on the floor, looking at his phone. DREW enters carrying a shoebox.

DREW:	OK, it was mostly junk in that dresser but I found this box of old photos. I think if we move some furniture out of there, potential buyers could see how big that front bedroom really is.
BRETT:	*(Looking at his phone.)* Do I know a Carrie Van Bilsen?
DREW:	I don't know...do you?
BRETT:	She just sent me a friend request but her profile picture is a cat. It's called Facebook, Carrie, not catbook.
DREW:	I thought you were cleaning out that cupboard.
BRETT:	I am. Should I accept her?
DREW:	We're only here for five days, Brett, can we use this time wisely? Do you think your dad would want these photos?
BRETT:	Maybe. Oh, Carrie!
DREW:	Where should I put them?
BRETT:	She's the one from the funeral. She changed her last name. I worked with her scooping ice cream one summer, but then she got pregnant. Oh and she sent me a message:
D/CARRIE:	*(Her Facebook message.)* Oh my God, Brett! So great to see you a couple weeks ago, LOL! Wish it could

	have been under happier circumstances. Sad face. OK, I hate doing business on Facebook, winky face, but word around town is you're planning on selling Maggie's house. I'm in real estate now so if you want to chat, my number is—
BRETT:	*(On his cell, leaving a message.)* Hey Carrie, Brett Brooks here. Whenever you get this, give me a shout back. I just got your note. We're actually in town till Tuesday so let's figure out a time to meet up.
DREW:	What about listing with Ray?
BRETT:	I know he's your friend—
DREW:	Our friend.
BRETT:	But she has to know the market out here better than he does. I just want to pick her brain.
DREW:	Fine. So…are we keeping these photos?
BRETT:	What are they?
DREW:	I don't know, it's your family. *(DREW looks at them.)* Is this the guy who built this place?
BRETT:	Let me see? Yeah. My great-great grandpa. He was the one who made all the money with the ships going back and forth to the States. And…these are his sons…that one's my great grandpa and that's his brother who lost the family fortune.
DREW:	He's the one who went to jail?
BRETT:	As my family puts it, "For a business misunderstanding."
DREW:	More commonly known as, "Rum Running."
BRETT:	He didn't know what was on those boats!
DREW:	The Brooks family! Experts at denial since 1927! You look like him. Handsome. Who's this?

Bed and Breakfast

BRETT: That's my grandma and grandpa with my dad as a boy and that baby is Aunt Maggie. And that's my parents' wedding. Oh, those poor bridesmaids. They must have got those dresses the same year they got these curtains.

DREW: Is this Maggie?

BRETT: Ha! Yeah! Oh man, look at her.

DREW: I thought she couldn't have kids.

BRETT: No, she couldn't. She's not actually pregnant, it's a Halloween costume, there's a jack-o'-lantern, see?

DREW: She dressed up as the pregnant Virgin Mary for Halloween?

BRETT: I guess. That's hilarious—she always had the funniest costumes. She didn't know she couldn't have kids until she got married and they started trying. See, that's her wedding. The marriage only lasted a few years, I barely remember him.

DREW: Is this you!?

BRETT: Ahhh! Give me that!

DREW: What are you doing?

BRETT: I'm dying Maggie's hair.

DREW: You look like you should be in a boy band.

BRETT: Shut up!

DREW: And this Celine Dion T-shirt?! You said your family was surprised when you came out.

BRETT: They were!

DREW: Oh, sweetie. They were lying.

Shift. A montage.

BRETT: *(On the phone.)* Hi there, is this the Goodwill? What are your hours? We have a lot to donate.

DREW: *(To BRETT.)* Hey, what do you want to do for dinner? Do you want to get groceries and cook together like old times?

BRETT: *(Watching TV.)* This show is terrible.

DREW: I know.

BRETT: I love it.

DREW: Me too.

BRETT: *(Going to bed.)* Good night, Mister.

DREW: Good night, Mister.

BRETT: *(Getting up.)* Whoa…you're up early.

DREW: I'm going for a run. I'm going to see if I can run more than two blocks here without hacking up a lung. Wanna come?

BRETT: You couldn't pay me. I'm going to read the paper. Imagine—a paper made of actual paper.

DREW: *(To us.)* I run down Maggie's street, past all the other big old Victorian houses, down to the water—

BRETT: I sit with my coffee on the big wrap-around porch.

DREW: All the way to the other end of town. I turn and find myself in the neighbourhood they don't put on the postcards. Where the porch swings end and the porch couches begin.

BRETT: The old man across the street from Maggie's lets his dog out the front door the same time every morning. The first day, we wave politely. The second day, he says:

D/HAROLD: Good morning there.

BRETT: And by the third day, he calls across the street:

D/HAROLD: Brett, isn't it? Harold Henderson. Do you remember Angus?

BRETT: *(A dog barks gently.)* Angus!

DREW: Past the grocery store, the gas station, the hardware, and onto the main drag—a mix of things you find in every small town: barbershop, florist, couple of banks, the Chinese restaurant, the greasy spoon—and places you only find in towns like this one: the stained glass place, the antique store, the locally made ice cream, the shop that specializes in items for your "Cottage Lifestyle", which, as far as I can see, just means everything has a loon painted on it.

BRETT: The last summer I spent here, the people across the street—Harold Henderson and his wife—went away for a weekend and gave me twenty bucks to take care of their new puppy. And here he is now, his old hips creaking down their front steps. *(To the dog. Sounds of Angus panting.)* Hey Angus, how've you been, old boy? Have you been a good dog?

DREW: On the fourth morning, I run an extra block and almost run smack into—

Shift.

B/ALISON: Ahhh! Sorry! Sorry!

DREW: No, I'm sorry!

B/ALISON: No, I'm sorry. I wasn't looking where I was going. Sorry. I'm behind. I spent an hour with my head in the toilet. Morning sickness. The worst. Sorry.

DREW: Are you open?

B/ALISON: Sorry! I am! Open!

They enter ALISON's cafe and we hear the ding-ding of the bell above the door.

DREW: Cool place. Do you do lattes?

B/ALISON: The best lattes in town! Well, the only lattes in town really, but yes I do!

DREW: Great. Can I have a grande?

B/ALISON: Sorry. We don't have that here. I could make you a large…

DREW: A large would be perfect.

B/ALISON: From Toronto?

DREW: Is it that obvious?

B/ALISON: You on vacation?

DREW: No, I'm—we're—just in town for the week to clean up a house, put it on the market.

B/ALISON: Oh yeah, whereabouts?

DREW: Just up Queen Street there. *(He points…and she points the right way.)* There. Corner of Queen and George.

B/ALISON: Maggie's place? Oh, we're going to miss her. What a shock.

DREW: Yeah.

B/ALISON: Brett spoke at the funeral, right? So you must be…

DREW: Drew.

B/ALISON: Drew! Yes! Sorry. Hey Drew, I'm Alison. *(They shake hands.)* Oh, did I get milk on you? Sorry. OK, so one latte, that's three dollars.

DREW: Three dollars?

B/ALISON: I know. Sorry. Small business.

DREW: No, no. *(Reaching for his wallet.)* Shit...I was running, I don't have my wallet.

B/ALISON: That's OK.

DREW: No, I will run home and grab it and run right back and—

B/ALISON: Sorry, no. Last summer, for my and Chris's wedding, Maggie did my hair. And I was complaining about how the yellow roses for the boutonnieres didn't match the bridesmaid dresses. Sorry, I know. But she went home, cut honest to God every single rose from her garden, brought them back, the perfect colour, dozens of them. We only needed four. So in the spirit of that generosity, there you go. *(She hands him the latte.)*

DREW: I will get you back.

B/ALISON: Don't worry about it.

DREW: Thanks, Alison. It was nice...running into you! Mmm...this is good.

BRETT: *(To us.)* And on the fifth morning, right on time, Harold Henderson's door opens, Angus waddles down his steps, looks both ways to cross the street, walks up onto the porch, sits down beside me and grants me permission to pet him until he decides it's time we both get on with our day.

Shift.

D/CARRIE: Oh my God! They sure don't build 'em like this anymore, do they?

BRETT: They sure don't.

D/CARRIE: Look at those baseboards. *(She measures the size between two fingers and holds it up.)* What is that? Eight inches? Eight and a half?

BRETT: (*Beat.*) So Carrie...what do you think?

D/CARRIE: Oh my God, I'm just going to tell you the truth. We could try and list it now, but it's the wrong time of year, tourist season is pretty much over, it would sit on the market with no interest for months, maybe years. It's charming, but it's a really huge, really old house, and it needs a ton of work.

BRETT: So what do you suggest we do?

D/CARRIE: Move in? Oh my God, imagine! But honestly, your best hope is a buyer who wants to convert it into something, but it could be a long time before that person comes along.

BRETT: Wow. Thanks for the honesty.

D/CARRIE: Oh my God, I don't mean to discourage you. Think it over, be in touch. And sometime you're back in town, you should come over. I'd love you to meet Dustin. But stay off the streets! He just got his beginners.

BRETT: Whoa! Time flies! Are you still with—

D/CARRIE: His dad? Oh my God no.

BRETT: Well, thanks for coming by, Carrie.

D/CARRIE: Anytime! See you on Facebook!

DREW: (*To us.*) Toronto!

Shift. Sounds of Toronto.

B/JEFFREY: Next!

DREW: Good morning, Jeffrey, how are you today?

B/JEFFREY: Can I take your order?

DREW: Grande latte, please.

B/JEFFREY: Your name?

DREW: (*Beat.*) How long have you worked here, Jeffrey?

B/JEFFREY: Four years. Name?

DREW: And in that four years, how many times do you figure I've come in here?

B/JEFFREY: We have a lot of regulars. That's five fifteen.

DREW: Did the price go up?

B/JEFFREY: Yes. Swipe towards me.

DREW: I know, Jeffrey.

B/JEFFREY: Your beverage will be at the end.

DREW: I know!

B/JEFFREY: Have a good day...Drew.

Shift. Split scene again, TV and work.

DREW: (*Answering a ringing phone.*) Good morning, front desk.

BRETT: Our first question today comes from Joe.

DREW: (*Holding a hand over the receiver.*) Hey Britney, is there a reason you double-charged these people's credit card?

BRETT: Joe just bought a house right here in Toronto and he's about to start a major renovation.

DREW: (*To a customer.*) OK, sir, good news.

BRETT: Let's look at the pictures of Joe's place.

DREW: I pulled a few strings and I got you two tickets for tonight at eight.

BRETT: There's the living room—

DREW: No, I haven't seen it.

BRETT:	And there's the kitchen.
DREW:	But I hear it's very good.
BRETT:	Wait a minute. This looks familiar.
DREW:	*(A phone is ringing.)* Britney…
BRETT:	Well, Joe…I—uh—
DREW:	Britney, are you going to answer that?
˙BRETT:	I have to admit I've been in your place before.
DREW:	*(She's not.)* Front desk.
BRETT:	Me and my uh—
DREW:	Oh, hey Wesley.
BRETT:	I put an offer on this place. But it looks like you got it.
DREW:	Oh, my days off were great, thanks.
BRETT:	So…congratulations.
DREW:	You have exciting news? Well, that's…
BRETT:	As for your question…
DREW:	Exciting!
BRETT:	I can tell you what I would have done.

Shift. DREW enters the condo.

BRETT:	You're home late. Did you eat?
DREW:	I grabbed some street meat. The subway was down, so I walked to College and got on the streetcar but traffic was so bad it didn't move, so I got off and walked the rest of the way. But it started raining halfway and then that lady on the corner screamed at me again.

BRETT: What was it about this time?

DREW: I don't know. I keep trying to tell her I don't speak Portuguese. Do we have any Tums?

BRETT: In there.

DREW goes to another room. Beat. From "off":

DREW: They gave it to Britney.

BRETT: What?

DREW: The promotion. unsatisfactory jobs

BRETT: What!?

DREW: (Re-entering.) I can't work there anymore.

BRETT: I know. (Beat:) Growing up, all I ever wanted to do was live in Toronto and now…I'm not so sure. ✱

DREW: Me neither.

BRETT: What if we did what Carrie said?

DREW: What?

BRETT: Move in.

DREW: To Maggie's?

BRETT: We are looking for a house…

DREW: She was kidding.

BRETT: Yeah. So am I.

DREW: (Beat.) You have always said you want a project.

BRETT: That house is too big for us. And what would we do out there?

DREW: Open a Bed and Breakfast?

BRETT: Ha! Yeah right!

DREW: No. Wait. You can design it. I could run that kind of business in my sleep.

BRETT: I can make eggs. You can make coffee.

DREW: How hard can it be? *foreshadow!*

BRETT: I love it there.

DREW: Me too. I love it there. I hate it here.

BRETT: Me too. Oh God, are we actually talking about this?

DREW: We're not talking about it. We're doing it.

Shift.

B/RAY: Girl, what is the one thing I told you not to do?

DREW: It's going to be great, Ray. We're going to renovate and open a B and B.

B/RAY: This is a joke, right? You two moving to a small town and going all floral wallpaper and English breakfast tea on me?

DREW: It'll be great for us. So we need to list the condo.

B/RAY: You're giving up your place in the city?

DREW: We need the money for the reno.

B/RAY: Do you have any friends out there?

DREW: Yes. Brett knows people. Sort of.

B/RAY: What are you going to do with yourselves? There's no bars, no clubs, no culture.

DREW: Ray, we haven't been to a club in years. We haven't been to any "culture" in months. We're so busy trying to afford to live here that we don't actually do any living here. This decision is about quality of life.

B/RAY: And what kind of quality of life do gay people have in this town?

DREW: We'll find out. I refuse to go into this assuming that everyone hates me.

B/RAY: Don't go into it assuming everyone loves you either. Here in the city, you and Brett fly a bit more under the gaydar than some of us, but out there, you two will be very, conspicuously, flamingly gay.

DREW: Thank you for the words of encouragement, Raymond.

B/RAY: Don't disappear on me, girl.

DREW: If we get desperate to see a drag queen, we can always hop on the 401 and stay with you.

B/RAY: Bitch.

DREW: I mean—

B/RAY: I know. So. Let's do this thing.

Shift. To us:

DREW: Thursday: the listing goes up.

BRETT: Saturday: a full-blown bidding war.

DREW: We have become the people we hate.

BRETT: Monday: the winning bid is a quick closing.

DREW: Extremely quick. Thursday:

BRETT: We hit the road.

DREW: One cube van.

BRETT: One car load. Our little two vehicle convoy heads out of town.

DREW: We're like pioneers!

BRETT: Two vehicles full of Banana Republic button-down shirts and back issues of *Better Homes and Gardens*!

DREW: Like gay pioneers!

BRETT: The renovations at Maggie's place—our place—start right away.

DREW: A complete gut-job.

BRETT: And when you want the job done right, you call—

Shift. Demolition and renovation sounds under this scene.

BRETT: Hey Doug, this isn't a load-bearing wall, is it?

D/DOUG: One way to find out.

BRETT: I hope there's exposed brick under here.

D/DOUG: Oh yeah.

BRETT: I'd love to have a feature wall.

D/DOUG: Oh yeah. Danny, Sean, go easy on those—somebody could use 'em.

BRETT: Really? Those cabinet doors are so dated.

D/DOUG: Oh. Yeah? *(He shares a not-so-covert limp wrist with Danny and Sean.)* ✶ homophobia

BRETT: Never mind.

DREW: *(Entering.)* Hey sweetie, that wallpaper in our bedroom is just peeling off in tiny bits.

BRETT: Do we have any fabric softener?

DREW: Um, we have dryer sheets.

BRETT: No, if you sponge liquid fabric softener on the paper, it peels off easier.

DREW: Huh! I'll go get some. Do you want the Mountain Air one or the Lavender?

BRETT: Whatever.

DREW: Anybody want anything from Alison's while I'm out? Danny? Sean?

BRETT: You want a coffee, Doug?

D/DOUG: Don't need nothing from that place.

BRETT: She has regular coffee if that's what you want, Doug...

DREW: What about you? Do you want that vanilla bean macchiato thing you like?

BRETT: Uh...whatever.

DREW: Do you want non-fat?

BRETT: I don't care, OK?! Just get me whatever!

DREW: OK... I'll be back in a bit.

BRETT: Yep. Bye.

DREW goes in for a kiss, BRETT dodges it, checking to see how DOUG and the guys react.

Shift. The ding-ding of the bell at ALISON's cafe.

B/ALISON: Hey Drew! Do my boobs look bigger to you?

DREW: Umm....hi Alison. I'm probably not the right person to ask.

B/ALISON: Ha! Sorry! Right. This morning, Chris swore they looked bigger. Did you guys start your reno yet?

DREW: Yeah, they're ripping out the kitchen today. Hey, do you know our contractor, Doug?

B/ALISON: Bigger guy? Older? Beard? I know who he is...

DREW: And those guys Danny and Sean who work for him?

B/ALISON: Not really, sorry, they were a bunch of grades below me.

DREW: But they're OK, right?

B/ALISON: Well, they're sort of rough around the edges. Why?

DREW: Brett's just acting weird. Like he didn't want me to kiss him goodbye in front of them.

B/ALISON: Oh, some people just don't like public displays of affection, you know? Chris is all for it, but sometimes I'm just like, "Sorry! Keep your hands to yourself!" Hey, what are you guys doing on Sunday?

DREW: Probably just working on the house.

B/ALISON: Here, here's our number. Give us a call. You should swing by. I want you to meet Chris—I think you guys'll hit it off. So what'll it be? Grande latte?

Shift.

DREW: I am just asking a question!

BRETT: It's not a big deal, Drew. * internalized homophobia

DREW: So if it's not a big deal, tell me why you did that.

BRETT: We can't just assume Doug and the guys are OK with it. It might freak them out.

DREW: I was giving you a kiss goodbye. I wasn't suggesting we have sex in front of them.

BRETT: I just doubt they've ever seen two men kiss before.

DREW: Well, no time like the present.

BRETT: But we're on their turf.

DREW: I'm pretty sure this is our turf. They work for us. In our house. It's not as if they think we're roommates, Brett.

BRETT: All I'm saying is not everyone in the world loves gay people.

DREW: Oh really? Thanks! I had no idea.

BRETT: Sorry, I know. But you didn't grow up here.

DREW: Technically neither did you.

BRETT: OK, look! I can tell Doug isn't completely comfortable around us, so—

DREW: We can find a new contractor.

BRETT: No, we can't. He's good. We just need to give him—give everybody—a bit of time, a bit of space, make sure they're cool before we make out in front of them.

DREW: A little peck is not making out! And I didn't quit my job, uproot my whole life, and move out here just to go back into the closet.

BRETT: But we can't pretend like it's not different. We can't just go about our lives in exactly the same way. There are no other gay people here.

DREW: OK, you know that can't be true, right?

BRETT: Where are they?

DREW: That guy at the Chinese restaurant is super friendly.

BRETT: Because we're the only people who go in there. The point is, even if they exist, they don't go around shoving it in people's faces.

DREW: Whoa! Can you hear yourself? That is like the catchphrase of homophobes who won't admit to being homophobes: "I'm fine with it as long as they don't shove it in my face." "I have no problem with you being gay as long as I don't have to see it."

BRETT: I'm just suggesting we use a little discretion, OK?

DREW: No Brett, you're suggesting we hide. Change the way we live to make people who don't even like us comfortable. I won't do it!

BRETT: Well for your own safety, you might have to!

DREW: *(Beat.)* What?

BRETT: Nothing.

DREW: Brett…

BRETT: *(Beat.)* Yesterday, I was turning left out of the grocery store and there was this transport truck parked in the way. So I pulled out in front of someone. He slammed on his brakes, it was fine.

DREW: There should be a stop light there.

BRETT: I waved at him like, "My mistake," and kept going. But he gets in the other lane, honking, pointing for me to pull over, gets out of his car, comes up to my window and screams, "Why don't you look where you're going, you cocksucker?"

DREW: Well, that's mature. But it's not like he meant—

BRETT: And then he says, "Why don't you and the other faggot go back to where you came from?"

DREW: Oh. But. This is where you came from. *homophobic

BRETT: Technically, it's not.

Shift. Two dogs barking.

140 *Bed and Breakfast*

B/ALISON: Sorry guys! Murray, KD, settle down, you two! Sorry, they get excited about new people. Hi guys. Sorry!

DREW: Hey Alison.

BRETT: *(To a dog.)* Are you Murray? Are you a good dog? Who's a good dog, Murray?

DREW: It's beautiful out here, Alison. How far back does your property go?

B/ALISON: Back to those trees. Oh wow, they're really changing colour now. We actually got this place for the shed, for Chris's business.

DREW: Oh yeah, what's that?

Sounds of a motorbike driving toward them.

B/ALISON: Small engine repair. Speak of the devil. Chris just ran to The LCBO before they close. We were dry.

DREW: *(To us.)* Chris pulls up on a really cool vintage motorbike. Leather jacket, boots, tight jeans—

BRETT: Gets off, swaggers one hell of a swagger up to Alison, rips off the helmet, lays a kiss on her and says:

D/CHRIS: How's my little Mama doing? Now, which one of you lads is which? Brett, right? We saw you at the funeral.

BRETT: *(Handshake. Chris has a very firm grip.)* Yes, hi. I uh—I didn't realize you were—uhhh— *presumptuous*

D/CHRIS: Irish.

BRETT: A woman, a lesbian, a lesbian woman. Drew didn't tell me.

DREW: I didn't know! And so Alison, I guess that makes you a lesbian, a woman, a woman lesbian too.

BRETT: Yeah Drew, that's how it works. So…Chris…when did you come to Canada?

D/CHRIS: Ten, twelve years ago, on a work visa, looking for a place where it didn't rain everyday.

BRETT: Did you go to Toronto?

D/CHRIS: Vancouver. Should have read up more on the weather, but this one was there for uni and the rest, as they say, is herstory. Ally, where are your shoes? Get inside, woman, before you freeze! You are literally barefoot and pregnant. *(More barking as they go inside.)* Settle down, KD. Murray, settle down girl.

BRETT: Oh, Murray's a girl?

D/CHRIS: Well, I sure hope so…she's pregnant. Alison's not the only bitch knocked up in this house, is she Murray?

B/ALISON: Christine! Sorry. It was a bit of an unplanned pregnancy—wasn't it, Murray? We looked out that window one day and she was going at it with the dog from three farms down.

D/CHRIS: Hell of a lot cheaper than how we did it, I'll tell you that. Know anybody who wants a puppy?

BRETT: Funny you should ask because—

DREW: Brett. We are not renovating a house and getting a puppy at the same time.

BRETT: Yeah but—

DREW: Don't even think about it, Mister.

               A bit more barking.

B/ALISON: Murray, sorry, we are talking about you. Come on, go outside, get outside, Anne Murray.

DREW: Anne Murray?

B/ALISON: That's her full name. And k.d. lang. Named after our favourite Canadian lesbians. And sorry, but before you say it, we know, Anne Murray isn't actually a lesbian.

D/CHRIS: But she is in my dreams, lads. She is in my dreams... Now, who needs a beer?

B/ALISON: I'll just have water...again. Hey! Sorry! You guys don't have a kitchen! Why don't you stay for supper?

DREW: *(To us.)* As the evening goes on, the conversation shifts away from dog breeds and espresso makers to—

BRETT: *(In scene.)* I have to ask: how do you two find it here? We're just trying to figure out living here and being gay.

D/CHRIS: Hold the phone...you two lads are gay?

B/ALISON: Christine. Sorry. She's like this all the time. Well, I grew up here, my parents live around the corner, my sister and her husband and their boys live in town, aunts, uncles, cousins, everybody. It's home, you know? It's where I want to live, where I want my kids to grow up. I'm not saying it's always easy...

D/CHRIS: I just miss being anonymous. I guess you give that up as the big, scary, Irish dyke on a bike who corrupted a sweet little hometown girl.

B/ALISON: Sorry, but I was already corrupted by the time I met you.

D/CHRIS: There was this one time at the pub. We went to see a band and the place was packed. I popped downstairs to the ladies' room and on my way out, there were a couple of lads waiting for me—young

*homophobic

guys, drunk. They pulled me into the men's washroom, pushed me up against the urinals. "Are you sure you were in the right bathroom? It says Ladies, you think you're a lady? If you're going to dress and act like a man, let's see you piss standing up." I was scared shitless—I may act tough, but I had no clue what to do. Luckily some other guy came in to take a piss and it all just sort of broke up. It could have gone much worse—these things usually do. But here's the thing: this summer, I was out on my bike and I came across a man and a little girl on the side of the road next to a four-wheeler. I pulled over to see if they needed help and I recognized him. He was one of those lads from the pub. I don't know if he could tell I remembered him, doesn't matter, it was a really simple fix on the ATV, just a wire that came loose, and this little girl, his daughter, probably five, six years old watches me fix it, really intently, and finally says, "Are you a boy or a girl?" And I turn, ready to lay into her about what a rude question that is, and I look her in the eye, and I see she's really asking the question. Just curious, just asking. So I say, "I know I have short hair and I'm wearing this leather jacket and it's sort of confusing, but I'm a girl. Do you know how some days you like to wear a fancy dress and some days you like to wear your jeans? Well, ninety-nine point nine percent of the time, I'm more of a jeans girl." And without skipping a beat, she says, "I got purple jeans last year for Christmas. Purple's my favourite colour." And the guy, her dad, he says thanks, and they go on their way. I don't know. I think that's something.

B/ALISON: Yeah, mama…I think that's something.

Shift. Doorbell. DREW answers the door.

DREW: Hello.

B/DUSTIN: Like, you're not Brett.

DREW: No, I'm Drew.

B/DUSTIN: Is Brett like home?

DREW: No, he's out. Can I help you with something?

B/DUSTIN: I'm like supposed to deliver this to him. It's like a letter from the Downtown Business Association. My mom just told me to like drop it off after school. Carrie. Van Bilsen. Is like my Mom.

DREW: Oh! Are you Justin?

B/DUSTIN: Dustin. Like with a D. Like Hoffman, not like Bieber. My mom like saw some pictures on Facebook where Brett was like volunteering for like this parade in Toronto. Like the umm...

DREW: The Pride Parade?

B/DUSTIN: Yeah. Like I think so, yeah.

DREW: Do you want to come in? *(DUSTIN does.)* Brett just helped out on parade day because I made him. I was on the committee. So did your mom want you to come meet us because you're...

B/DUSTIN: No! No. She like needs your help. Like, Maggie always did it, like she organized everything and like my mom would help out and then I would like help my mom. But now, Maggie's like dead and you need somebody like super-organized, but like let's be serious, that's not really my mom, so she was like thinking of people to ask and then she like saw those pictures on Facebook and she was like, "Oh my God, this is perfect! Brett can do it!" But now like maybe you're the one we should be asking.

DREW: Asking...?

B/DUSTIN: Oh my God, Dustin, stop like rambling! The Santa Claus Parade? It's in like three weeks. It's happening, but we are like so unorganized and like so far behind this year. But you can like save us.

DREW: No no no, I was just on a committee.

B/DUSTIN: That's like way more experience than anybody else has.

DREW: Honestly Dustin, my job was just to make sure the Gay NDPs and the Gay Liberals didn't make fun of the Gay Conservatives. There were only three of them, but still...

B/DUSTIN: There's this like meeting on Thursday, 7:30, at Alison's Cafe. All the info's in there.

DREW: Why didn't your mom just call?

B/DUSTIN: I'm like not sure. Oh I like almost forgot, I like made you this pie.

DREW: You made a pie?

B/DUSTIN: I was like bored. So like see you at the meeting.

DREW: Oh, I didn't say that I would—

B/DUSTIN: *(Already fleeing.)* Thursday, OK?

DREW: Thursday.

    Shift.

BRETT: Thursday?

DREW: You have to come with me. Please?

BRETT: This Thursday? As in Thursday, November fourteenth?

DREW: Shit. Sorry. Can we celebrate on Friday? I really need your help with this.

BRETT: The last time we had this conversation, I wound up in a fight with the leader of a gay senior citizens' marching band who told me, and I quote, "Save your breath, Mary, we're so gay we can't even line up straight."

DREW: I cannot guarantee that won't happen again, but it's highly unlikely.

BRETT: I'm too busy with the house!

DREW: So am I! This is a great chance to get involved in the community. It'll be good for us.

BRETT: Drew. Look at this place. It looks like a bomb went off in here. I don't have time for this.

DREW: I'm sorry…are you saying you don't have time… for Santa?

Shift. Ding-ding.

B/ALISON: Hi everybody! Sorry! Sorry! Does anybody need a coffee or anything before we start?

D/CARRIE: Oh my God, Alison, yes! I'd take a tea!

BRETT: Non-fat Vanilla Machiatto. Double.

DREW: Large latte. The usual.

B/DUSTIN: Can I like have a peppermint mocha hot chocolate?

DREW: OK! Everybody good? This meeting is, as they say, in session.

B/ALISON: Sorry, can I go? Sorry. Our main concern this year is who's going to be Santa. For the past ten years, Dennis Podemski has done it, but they go to Florida earlier every year so he'll be away by the first weekend in December.

DREW: Well, how did he get to be Santa?

B/ALISON: Sorry, I was still in Vancouver. There was some sort of a contest, wasn't there?

D/CARRIE:	Oh my God, Santa Idol! That was a hoot. We should do that.
B/DUSTIN:	Oh! Like, also, I like brought cupcakes. *(He pulls them out.)*
DREW:	OK Dustin, thank you. So this Santa Idol thing—
B/DUSTIN:	Mom said it's like Brett's birthday—
D/CARRIE:	Oh my God Brett, I saw it on Facebook.
B/DUSTIN:	So I made cupcakes when I got home from school. There's like two kinds—double chocolate with peanut butter cream cheese icing—allergy alert everybody!—and coconut with mango glaze. So. Like. Happy birthday!
D/CARRIE:	Oh my God, try losing weight with this one around.
BRETT:	That's really nice of you, Dustin. We loved your pie.
DREW:	Yes, thanks, so getting back to the—
B/ALISON:	*(Sings.)* Happy birthday to you! Happy bir— Sorry! Sorry.
DREW:	Back to Santa—do we have time to do a contest? This thing's coming up.
B/ALISON:	Sorry. You're probably right. Who do we know who could be Santa?
D/CARRIE:	Oh my God, what about Don Wigaboltis? He used to do it before Dennis. Smoking his pipe and everything.
B/ALISON:	Sorry, no! He's on oxygen now.
DREW:	OK, we don't have to answer this right now, let's just ask around, come up with some names, keep in touch via email—

B/ALISON: The other issue we're facing is promotion. Sorry, were you done? Attendance has really been down these past couple years and from the perspective of the Downtown Business Association, the main reason for doing this is to get people out and shopping downtown.

D/CARRIE: Oh my God, Dustin, how many points would one of these be?

B/DUSTIN: Like...a lot.

DREW: OK everybody, can we try to focus—

BRETT: Drew didn't get me a cake this year, Dustin, so I really appreciate this.

DREW: OK! Alison, you were saying...

B/ALISON: Sorry. Maggie could usually get a story in the paper but I called Stewart about it today, and he said they do the same article every year and it feels like we're asking for free advertising. He asked, "What's the angle?"

D/CARRIE: Oh my God, Stewart! It's a community event, there is no angle, just write the article.

B/DUSTIN: Mom.

D/CARRIE: What?

B/DUSTIN: I'll talk to him. Stewart is like...my dad.

DREW: OK great! Moving on to the next thing on the list—

BRETT: *(A mouthful of cupcake.)* Mmm! Dustin, this cupcake is incredible.

DREW: Moving on!

Shift. BRETT runs over to the side of the house.

BRETT:	Wait wait wait wait wait wait wait. *(He plugs in the Christmas lights and calls out.)* Is it working? How do they look?
DREW:	Wow. What is this going to do to the hydro bill?
BRETT:	*(Joining him.)* I think after six years of living in the condo, I might have got a bit carried away…
DREW:	How many trees had to die to make that wreath? It's enormous.
BRETT:	It's a big front door. It's about proportion. But you have to admit…
DREW:	It looks beautiful.
BRETT:	It needs snow.

A pause as they look at the house. DREW sighs.

BRETT:	What's up?
DREW:	Nothing. Christmas. Makes me miss my family.
BRETT:	I know.
DREW:	It's so stupid. I sent my parents a Christmas card extra extra early so they'd have my new return address, just in case this is the year they decide to write me back. Thirteen years this Christmas. How long do you hold out hope that someone's going to come around?
BRETT:	I don't know.
DREW:	I never really thought about it until Maggie died, but what if one of them is gone and no one got in touch to tell me?
BRETT:	Don't you think your sister would call?
DREW:	I don't know. She's as bad as they are.
BRETT:	*(Beat.)* You know what?

DREW: What?

BRETT: Their loss, Mister.

DREW: Yeah, Mister. Their loss.

Shift. The home phone rings. BRETT answers.

BRETT: Hello? Hello?...Hello? *(He hangs up and gets back to work on the house.)*

D/DOUG: *(Entering.)* All that tile's on back-order so we can't do nothing on the bathrooms for another week, probably two.

BRETT: What?! The tile was supposed to come in today, Doug.

D/DOUG: Got screwed up. You ordered too much.

BRETT: Because we're doing five washrooms!

D/DOUG: At the same time. Each one with about three goddamn different tiles.

BRETT: Where are we supposed to shower for the next two weeks, Doug?

D/DOUG: Shoulda thought of that before you made me rip everything out. Least we kept the one toilet.

BRETT: Yeah, it's a real pleasure sharing a toilet with you and Danny and Sean.

D/DOUG: Ever think how we feel sharing it with the two of you?

BRETT: What is that supposed to mean? Doug, look. This is my house. My and Drew's house. So I'm going to have to ask you to cut that out.

D/DOUG: You wanna hire somebody else?

BRETT: You said business was dead. I'm trying to help you out.

D/DOUG: Don't need help from you.

BRETT: Then what are you doing here?! *(Beat.)* Have you thought about what Drew asked you?

D/DOUG: Thought about it. Answer is no.

BRETT: We just thought it might be good for you.

D/DOUG: Oh yeah? You know what's good for me now?

BRETT: Guess I don't.

D/DOUG: Fine.

BRETT: Fine. *(Beat.)* All you have to do is sit on the sleigh and wave at people.

D/DOUG: I don't wear costumes.

BRETT: But you're perfect for it.

D/DOUG: You know, that ain't exactly a compliment.

BRETT: We just thought you might want to help out. In memory of Maggie. It sounds like this was her baby. *(DOUG looks at him.)* The Santa Claus Parade, Doug.

D/DOUG: I'll pass. *(He starts to exit.)*

BRETT: You know, we're just regular people, Doug. Just like anybody else.

D/DOUG: So like regular people who order fifteen fancy tiles for your five bathrooms, you can wait two weeks to get it.

> Shift. BRETT and DREW get their photo taken. As the picture is snapped, DREW throws his arm around BRETT.

BRETT & DREW: Cheese!

BRETT: "Brett Brooks (brackets) left, nephew of the late Margaret 'Maggie' Brooks—

DREW: "And Drew Lazarenko (brackets) right, are hard at work turning their century home at Queen and George into what they describe as—

BRETT: "A chic and modern country getaway."

DREW: "The newcomers from Toronto are already involved in the community—

BRETT: "Helping to organize this Friday evening's—"

Shift.

DREW: OK! Alison and Brett, you two will line everything up down at this end. Carrie, Dustin, it's up to you to keep things moving further down Main Street. If the Shriners or the bagpipers want to stop, that's fine, but only for a minute. And now, after exhausting all of our other options, let's have a round of applause for our Santa! *(Applause.)*

BRETT: Woo! I didn't think it would work, but you look perfect!

D/CHRIS: As a little girl growing up in Dublin, never in my wildest dreams did I imagine one day I'd be wearing a fat suit and fake beard waiting to be pulled through a small town in Canada on a flatbed truck. Today is a very unique day. Now! Let's have ourselves a parade!

Shift. Sounds of the parade. To us:

BRETT: Floats from churches, businesses, service groups—

DREW: The high school choir, the Legion, classic cars from every decade—

BRETT: Little Sunday school kids on a hay wagon dressed up as the most adorable Nativity I have ever seen.

D/CARRIE: *(In scene.)* Oh my God, this is the best turn-out we've had in years!

B/DUSTIN: They must have like read about it in the paper.

DREW: *(Back to us.)* People from neighbouring towns, parents, grandparents, teenagers, little kids—

BRETT: A pregnant lesbian *(Sings.)* and a partridge in a pear tree!

DREW: This! Is!

BRETT & DREW: Awesome!

DREW: When all the vacationers are far away, when nobody will even dip a toe into the water for another six months, these are the people who live here—

BRETT: People who were born here and people, like us, who have chosen to call this place...well, to call it home.

D/CHRIS: *(From the float.)* Ho! Ho! Ho! Merry Christmas! Ho! Ho! Ho!

B/LITTLE GIRL: It's the real Santa! It's not the fake one like in my Wal-Mart picture, Dad! This is the real Santa! SANTA! SANTA! I WANT ANOTHER PAIR OF PURPLE JEANS!!!

Shift. Parade sounds fade out. BRETT and DREW walk home.

DREW: Well, I would call that a success. Thanks for helping.

BRETT: My pleasure. Hey, look... *(It snows.)* What do you want for Christmas?

DREW: I want this renovation to be over. I want to never eat take-out Chinese ever again. I want people to come to this bed and breakfast. You?

BRETT: Same as always.

DREW: I can't get you concert tickets if Celine Dion isn't on tour.

BRETT: The other thing.

DREW: We're in no rush. Someday, OK?

BRETT: No, you know what? No presents this year. How's that sound? I've got everything I need.

> BRETT *does a shoulder-check. He takes* DREW's *hand. They walk home in the snow.*

DREW: I thought you turned the Christmas lights on before we left.

BRETT: I did.

DREW: *(To us.)* As we get closer to the house, we see the wreath broken in the middle of the street—

BRETT: Cedar garland all over the yard—

DREW: Christmas lights hanging down, the wires cut and—

BRETT: *(In scene.)* Oh my God. Look.

DREW: Oh my God.

BRETT: *(To us.)* Spray painted across the front of the house, in big block letters:

BRETT & DREW: FAGGOTS, GO HOME.

[Handwritten annotation: CLIMAX!]

BRETT: A call to the police. A report filed. A promise they'll let us know if there are any other reports of vandalism.

Shift.

DREW: Vandalism!? This is more than vandalism! Doesn't this count as a hate crime?

BRETT: You heard what he said, they're taking it seriously but— Who cares what they call it, Drew!? *(He makes a call on his cell.)*

DREW: I care! What does it take to call it what it is? Who are you calling?

BRETT: My brother. We can go stay with him tonight.

DREW: What?

BRETT: Shit. *(Voicemail.)* Hey Steve, it's Brett, give me a call when you get this, OK?

DREW: Whoa. Hey. What are you doing?

BRETT: *(Dialling another number, he starts to get clothes out.)* My mom and dad will be home. We can go there. *(Voicemail again.)* Urrrrgh, come on. Hi, it's me, we're coming back towards Toronto, we need a place to stay tonight, call me back on my cell, OK? *(Hangs up.)* Can you call Ray? Maybe we can stay with him. Or we'll just get a hotel.

DREW: What are you talking about?

BRETT: What if they come back? It's not safe!

DREW: Brett, you're overreacting.

BRETT: Overreacting? I'm overreacting? To this? To THAT?

DREW: I know you're freaked out, but this stuff is usually a one-time thing just to scare people.

BRETT: *(Packing a bag.)* Well, it's working. And what if it's more than that?

DREW: Do you just want to get out of here for the night or—

BRETT: I tried, OK? I had my picture in the paper even though I didn't want to, I tried to talk to Doug, I tried not hiding and this is what happens.

DREW: Whoa, just calm down.

BRETT: Don't tell me to calm down! I thought this was what we wanted, but I can't do it. I can't live here.

DREW: Yes you can. Would you just stop and—

BRETT: I am scared, OK? I'm scared!

DREW: I know! I'm scared too! But we can't leave now.

BRETT: Why not?

DREW: Because. We can't let them win.

Blackout.

End of Act I.

Act II

> *In the dark, the sounds of a vehicle pulling up, parking, a car door, rustling. BRETT switches on his bedside lamp. Again, the two of them in bed.*

BRETT: Do you hear that? Hey. Drew.

DREW: *(Waking up.)* What?

BRETT: Did you hear that?

DREW: Hear what?

BRETT: That noise.

DREW: What time is it?

BRETT: *(Getting out of bed.)* Just after six. There's someone on the porch.

DREW: No there's not. Go back to sleep.

BRETT: I didn't sleep all night. I can't believe you slept.

DREW: You're just hearing things.

BRETT: *(Putting clothes on.)* I'm telling you there is someone down there.

DREW: Come back to bed.

> *A noise.*

BRETT: I told you. They came back. *(He exits the bedroom.)*

DREW: What are you doing? Brett?

BRETT arms himself with a broom or baseball bat. More noise. He bursts through the door, brandishing his weapon.

BRETT: GET OUT OF HERE! LEAVE US ALONE! AHHHHH!!!

D/CHRIS: AHHHHH! What in the hell do you think you're doing?

BRETT: Chris?

D/CHRIS: You scared me shitless! Put some boots on! Put a coat on! You're going to freeze to death!

BRETT: What are you doing out here?

D/CHRIS: Trying to get this hose hooked up, but it's frozen solid.

BRETT: What?

D/CHRIS: Well, I figured you lads wouldn't have a pressure washer and that's the only sure way to get this spray paint off the brick. I need some hot water to loosen this up. Now get inside before you catch cold and die. *(They move inside.)* So what are you lads going to do?

BRETT: What can we do? Drew's right—we've torn this place apart, all our money is tied up in it, we don't have jobs.

D/CHRIS: I mean about this. What did the police say?

BRETT: Oh, um— There's nothing to go on. I told them about this guy I had a run-in with on the street—I cut him off and he... But that was a couple months ago and I've never seen him around town again. It could have been anybody.

D/CHRIS: I've never been much of an activist, but a thing like this, especially when it happens to people I know, to my friends, it makes me want to fight back. But how, you know? Who do you fight? You'd think the people who'd do a thing like this—people with such strong opinions about us—wouldn't be such goddamn cowards. I've got a baby on the way, Brett. What kind of a screwed-up world is this kid coming into?

Shift. To us:

BRETT: So. It is one thing to tell you the story of how we came to live here—a story which is still incomplete...

DREW: Until all the cats are let out of all the bags. But even when we figure that out—

BRETT: How we ended up here—

DREW: We have a decision to make on the other side.

Shift. Doorbell. DREW answers it.

B/DUSTIN: It's not like too early, is it?

DREW: No, Dustin, hi, we've been up for a couple hours.

B/DUSTIN: I like...brought you guys cinnamon buns. I like couldn't sleep.

DREW: You didn't have to do that.

B/DUSTIN: I like wanted to. My dad like texted me a picture last night and like told me what happened. He like had to come by for the newspaper.

DREW: Do you want to come in?

B/DUSTIN: *(He does.)* So like when I heard, I was like really upset. Like— *(Shift.)* Can we just drive over there, Mom? I have to see it.

D/CARRIE: Oh my God, Dustin, no you don't.

B/DUSTIN: This is like all my fault! I like told Dad to put Drew and Brett in the paper for the parade. That's how the people who did this knew they weren't at home!

D/CARRIE: Oh my God, Dustin, this isn't your fault. Take a breath.

B/DUSTIN: No, Mom! You don't get it!

D/CARRIE: What don't I get?

B/DUSTIN: What it's like! I tell myself if I ignore it, it'll like stop, but it doesn't. Everybody makes fun of me. Every single day. They like call me a fag, push me in the hall—

D/CARRIE: Oh my God, honey, why didn't you—

B/DUSTIN: And Brett and Drew are like so cool. They are like really good people and I don't understand why somebody would do this to them, and I need to see it, because I'm like, "Is this just like how it's going to be? No matter what, no matter like how nice or how good I am, is it always going to be this hard?" Because like...I am...

D/CARRIE: *(Beat.)* Oh my God, Dustin. I love you. Your dad loves you. Nothing you can say is going to change that.

B/DUSTIN: I like...I think I'm gay.

D/CARRIE: *(Beat.)* I think you are too. Oh my God, Dustin, I've known since you were four years old.

Shift back to the scene with DREW.

B/DUSTIN: So like I guess I'm gay now. Like I guess I'm out. Of the like...closet.

DREW: That is the best news I've heard all day, Dustin. It's nicer out here.

B/DUSTIN: Is it?

DREW: I know this doesn't make it look very good, but...

B/DUSTIN: Please don't move away. At least not till like I'm done high school.

Shift. To us:

DREW: On Monday morning, at the bottom of the mailbox, an envelope without a stamp, addressed simply to Brett and Drew.

BRETT: Inside it, a Christmas card. And in perfect, if slightly shaky, handwriting:

D/HAROLD: Good morning, gentlemen. It upset me a great deal to see what happened to your house and your decorations. All of us on the street thought they looked lovely and helped to get us all into the festive spirit. We hope you replace them and we hope this helps.

BRETT: And a smaller envelope inside. Twenties, tens, fives, toonies. One hundred and eighty-six dollars.

D/HAROLD: Angus and I look forward to seeing the Christmas lights from our front window again soon. Most sincerely, Harold Henderson.

BRETT: PS.

D/HAROLD: Thank you for the parade.

BRETT: See over. *(Flips the card over.)*

D/HAROLD: I'm eighty-one years old, boys, and if there's one thing I've learned in my time on this earth, it's that:

D/HAROLD & BRETT: Love is stronger than hate.

Shift. Christmas music.

B/STEVE: Jesus H. Christ, Cody, save some room for dinner.

DREW: *(To us.)* Christmas in Oshawa.

B/STEVE: Do you have a hollow leg?

D/CODY: I dunno! I'm hungry, OK, Dad? Get off my back!

B/LYNDA: Steven, Cody, it's Christmas. Please, not in my house. Drew, would you give me a hand with this? In the kitchen…

DREW: Sure, Lynda. *(They go into the kitchen.)*

B/LYNDA: So. Drew. How are the two of you doing out there?

DREW: We're doing OK, thanks.

B/LYNDA: You can be honest, Drew. When Martin's parents passed away, he inherited that house, but I told him, we are not moving there, we are not living in that town, so he signed it over to Maggie. But when Brett said you two were moving out there, well I— Let's just say when we heard about this…incident, I wasn't exactly surprised. And three weeks later and nothing more from the police? You know you can always move back to Toronto. No one will think any less of you.

DREW: Thanks, Lynda. You said you needed some help?

> In addition to Christmas music, we hear CODY's music bleeding from his earphones.

BRETT: What did you get for Christmas, Cody? Cody? *(He lifts a headphone off CODY's ear. The volume increases.)* What did you get for Christmas?

D/CODY: I dunno. Stuff.

BRETT: How are your university applications going?

D/CODY: I dunno. OK, I guess. I'm applying for Poli-Sci. As far away from home as possible.

B/STEVE: Christ, Cody! I heard that! He's just applying everywhere his girlfriend is applying.

D/CODY: DAD! How many times do I have to tell you? We broke up!

BRETT: Sorry to hear that, Cody. You OK?

D/CODY: I dunno. Dad said if I want to move out, I have to make money this summer but I dunno, nobody in Oshawa will hire you without experience but you can't get experience unless you get a job.

BRETT: Yeah, that's a Catch-22, isn't it?

D/CODY: (*Beat.*) I dunno. I just thought…you know how you lived with Aunt Maggie in the summers and worked construction, well, maybe I could come and…I dunno…

BRETT: What? Live with us? Cody, we haven't even opened the B and B yet.

D/CODY: It's just…ever since Mom left, Dad and me don't really…I dunno. Please?

CODY's music out. Another Christmas song.

BRETT: Hey Dad, can I ask you something?

D/MARTIN: That depends on what it is you're asking.

BRETT: In that box of pictures I gave you, we found this photo of Maggie when she was young. See?

D/MARTIN: Looks like Halloween.

BRETT: Yeah, that's what I said, but I'm just checking if there's something I don't know.

D/MARTIN: Maggie couldn't have children.

BRETT: Yeah but she actually looks pregnant. Really pregnant.

D/MARTIN: Son, why do you insist on stirring everything up in this family?

BRETT: Somebody's got to.

D/MARTIN: Well, there's nothing to tell.

BRETT: Dad, I live out there. You can tell me the truth now or I can embarrass myself and Maggie and the whole family by not knowing later. Come on.

D/MARTIN: *(Beat.)* She was a teenager. Unmarried, of course. Your grandparents were having none of it. They dealt with it as they saw fit. Maggie went away. The baby was adopted. And years later, when she got married and they started trying, she couldn't conceive. *major event (knowledg of bb)

BRETT: I can't believe she never told me about this.

D/MARTIN: Your grandma and grandpa made us swear we'd never talk about it. So we never did. And we never will, all right, son? Let sleeping dogs lie.

BRETT: *(To us.)* That night. Back home.

Shift. Yet another Christmas song.

DREW: OK OK OK, I know we said we weren't doing presents—

BRETT: No! You cheated!?

DREW: I didn't want to do this at your parents' so I waited till we got home. In light of recent events, I've been thinking a lot about this and… I think maybe it's time. *(He pulls out a small jewelry-sized box and gives it to BRETT.)*

BRETT: Umm. Is this…?

DREW: Just open it.

BRETT: Oh my God. *(He opens it.)* OH MY GOD! Does this mean what I think it means?

DREW: Yes.

BRETT: Yes!

DREW: So...?

BRETT: YES!

DREW: That's just something to open. We'll get that dog tag engraved with the name once we pick it out.

BRETT: Where?

DREW: Chris and Alison's. Anne Murray had her puppies!

Shift.

BRETT: That one.

D/CHRIS: That one? The one in the corner? The runt?

BRETT: Yes. That's my dog.

D/CHRIS: Who am I to tell you different? Fair warning, though: he might need an extra couple weeks with his mum before he really gets going.

BRETT: That's OK. We'll wait for you, little guy.

DREW: What are we going to name him?

B/ALISON: Well, sorry, but we have this little rule about names—

DREW: Oh, it's a rule now?

B/ALISON: Sorry! OK, he has curly hair. He's little, but he's still pretty feisty. Umm... Sorry...

DREW: Umm...I got nothing. Brett?

BRETT: I got it. Rick Mercer.

D/CHRIS: Who the hell is that?

BRETT: Rick Mercer...you know, the guy who does the rants...on CBC?

D/CHRIS: Oh, him? But that guy's not gay. That's the rule.

BRETT: Yes he is. And Anne Murray is not.

D/CHRIS: Give her a night with me. *(To the dog.)* What do you say? You like the sound of that, little guy? You like that, Rick Mercer?

B/ALISON: *(The baby kicks.)* Oh! The baby approves! Ow! *(To her belly.)* Sorry!

> Shift. The landline phone rings. BRETT answers it. DREW is working on the computer.

BRETT: Hello? Hello?...Hello? *(He hangs up.)* Weird.

DREW: No one there?

BRETT: It sounded like someone was, but they hung up.

DREW: Great! It could have been someone trying to book a room. Our phone number is on B and B Canada now, but we're listed as "B and B TBA" and the way we answer the phone, it just sounds like you've called someone's house.

BRETT: When's the deadline to get us in that visitor's guide?

DREW: February first. Friday. If you're going to design a logo by then, we need a name. What did you come up with?

BRETT: *(Pulling out his list.)* Umm. Shady Maples.

DREW: That sounds...shady.

BRETT: Restful Shores.

DREW: Sounds like a nursing home.

BRETT: Country Slumbers.

DREW: That sounds like a cemetery!

BRETT: OK, I'll make the place look good, this isn't really my forte.

DREW: Well, maybe we should think outside the box. We're trying to make this place a bit more hip than most B and Bs, so the name could be something younger, less serious...

BRETT: Like...

DREW: Like... *(Reading from his list.)* Pillows and Pancakes.

BRETT: Young and hip, sure, but I don't think our main clientele will be thirteen-year-old girls at a sleepover.

DREW: OK fine, this is a good one: The Rumrunner's Rest.

BRETT: Oh, I'm sure my dad would love that.

DREW: OK OK OK, this one's my favourite. We're on the corner of Queen Street and George Street, so what about...The Queen George Inn?

BRETT: The Queen George Inn? Drew! That sounds like a gay bar in a Dickens novel.

DREW: I know! Isn't it perfect!?

BRETT: Let's keep thinking.

             Shift. BRETT is painting. DREW is on his cell phone.

D/DOUG: Son of a bitch. No, Danny, brushed nickel. *(To BRETT.)* That right?

BRETT: Right.

D/DOUG:	(*Phone.*) Four towel racks, brushed nickel. Well, ask if they have some in the back... Yeah, I'll wait...
BRETT:	(*Beat.*) Hey Doug? You and Maggie, you were friends, right? (*Beat.*) At Christmas, my dad told me she gave a baby up for adoption when she was a teenager.
D/DOUG:	Oh yeah?
BRETT:	Yeah, we found a picture of her dressed up for Halloween, pregnant out to here. I've been trying to get in touch with the baby—the person—and let them know that Maggie passed away, but you need to be the child in question or a birth parent for them to release certain information. Anyway, my dad doesn't know who the father was, or won't say, but I thought if you had any idea...?
D/DOUG:	I woulda already been married to Brenda when I was that age. I had no clue who was doing what with who.
BRETT:	Is there anyone who would know the father? A friend of hers from back then?
D/DOUG:	Doubt it. Most folks kept that kind of thing pretty under wraps 'round here.
BRETT:	Right.
D/DOUG:	What makes you think her kid wants you sticking your nose in their business anyway?
BRETT:	Well, I don't know... If they ever went looking for her, wouldn't it be easier if—
D/DOUG:	Don't sound like they've went looking for her up to now. And it don't sound like Maggie looked for them.
BRETT:	Yeah, but—

D/DOUG: Ever think that's the way she wanted it?

BRETT: *(Beat.)* Maybe you're right.

D/DOUG: Not everything needs to be out in the open. *(Phone.)* What's that, Danny? *(To BRETT.)* They're out of nickel, but they have stainless steel.

BRETT: They have to match the faucets.

D/DOUG: Wanna order 'em in? Here.

BRETT: *(On DOUG's phone.)* Hi Danny? Yeah, order four... Well, can you open an account there? ...Yes, Danny, the B and B finally has a name. Tell them to put it under—

Shift. A montage.

BRETT & DREW: Aunt Maggie's House Bed and Breakfast!

DREW: *(Answering the ringing landline.)* Aunt Maggie's House Bed and Breakfast, this is Drew.

BRETT: *(To a salesperson.)* Excuse me, hi, do you have these sheets in Queen Size?

DREW: What are the nights you'd like to book?

BRETT: *(At a door, to a little kid.)* Oh! Hello there. I'm the guy who called about the harvest table. Is your Mom home?

DREW: For the opening weekend? Great. I have a few options for you—

BRETT: *(At home.)* Whoa whoa whoa, Sean, that wallpaper goes the other way!

DREW: OK, you're all booked in. We'll see you in a couple weeks.

BRETT: *(Cell phone.)* Hi Doug? Do you think you could

	swing by this auction sale with the truck? I went a bit nuts.
DREW:	(Phone.) Aunt Maggie's House B and B, Drew speaking. Hello?... Hello? (Hangs up.)
BRETT:	(With the puppy.) No I know, Chris, and if it were up to me, I would've brought him home a month ago, but can you please just keep him for one more week?
DREW:	(Phone.) Aunt Maggie's House, this is Drew.
BRETT:	(Continued.) Drew just wants to get through this weekend.
DREW:	This weekend? Uhhh...yeah, it's actually our opening and we already have two bookings, but... the more the merrier.
BRETT:	(Another cell phone call, while baking.) No Mom, I don't understand your recipe. Do I need baking powder or baking soda? Is there a difference? (Doorbell.) Mom, I gotta go, I think the first guests are here. Thanks. Bye.
DREW:	(Meeting him at the front door.) Ready?
BRETT:	As I'll ever be.
	They open the door. Shift.
D/CHUCK:	Hello hello hello, I'm Charles, call me Chuck.
B/SHARON:	And I'm Sharon, call me Sharon. Oh! This is so exciting, isn't it, darling?! A little springtime anniversary getaway.
D/CHUCK:	Twenty-five years, three kids, and one move across the pond later.
B/SHARON:	Oh, this is charming! Did you say this is your first weekend? Are we...?

D/CHUCK: Popping your cherry?

B/SHARON: Chuck.

D/CHUCK: Wait a sec—Brett Brooks? Aren't you on telly? Yeah, I'd never forget that face.

Doorbell.

BRETT: Hello. Welcome. Are you Travis?

D/TRAVIS: Yo, sweet place, man. My girl Alexa thinks we're goin' back to our crib, but I was like, no man, we should stay someplace sweet, know what I'm sayin', for our wedding night.

BRETT: Well, we've put you in the front room, it's the closest thing we have to a honeymoon suite—

D/TRAVIS: Sweet man. A suite. That sounds sweet.

BRETT: Sweet. Since you'll be getting in late, I'll give you my cell number. Just text me when you're on your way and I'll let you in without ringing the doorbell and disrupting the other guests.

D/TRAVIS: Yo, man. Limo pulls up, door swings open, and booya, I'm gonna carry my girl Alexa over the threshold. Know what I'm sayin'? Sweet.

Doorbell!

B/SYLVIA: Well. This is certainly…different.

DREW: You must be Sylvia. When you booked on the phone, you mentioned you normally stayed at the Harbourview, is that right?

B/SYLVIA: The same weekend for over forty years. Ever since we've been having this annual regional meeting for PARTY.

DREW: PARTY? That sounds fun. What is that?

B/SYLVIA: It's an acronym for my organization. P.A.R.T.Y. Preaching Abstinence and Restraint To Youth.

DREW: Fun.

B/SYLVIA: I would still be at the Harbourview if it hadn't ceased operations. Shame. Though I don't expect you mind. But this is quite a bit more...modern than one is used to.

DREW: The idea was to do a slightly more contemporary style. I'm not really the right one to talk about it. My better half is the designer.

B/SYLVIA: Is she here?

DREW: No...he just ran to the store to get some baking powder. He'll be right back.

Shift. Late that night. Brett receives a text and tiptoes down the hall.

D/CHUCK: Hello, hello, hello.

BRETT: Ahh! Chuck, hello. You're up late. Is everything OK?

D/CHUCK: Better for seeing you. No, just one of those nights. A bit tossy-turny. Figured I'd pop out and let Sharon sleep. You?

BRETT: Oh, I'm just letting the last of the guests in— *(Doorbell.)* Shit. Sorry. Excuse me.

D/ALEXA: *(Her drunk wail outside the door.)* Where the hell are you taking me?

D/TRAVIS: Yo, shut up, Alexa, it's a surprise, OK?

BRETT: *(Opening the door. Sotto voce.)* Hello! Congratulations!

D/ALEXA: *(Forte.)* Who the hell are you?

BRETT:	I'm Brett. Welcome! The other guests are sleeping, so if you—
D/TRAVIS:	Yo baby, let me pick you up.
D/ALEXA:	You're not picking me up, you'll drop me, you're wasted.
D/TRAVIS:	Yo, I'M wasted? I'M wasted?!?
BRETT:	Shhh... OK. Beautiful dress.
D/ALEXA:	Travis! Stop it!
D/TRAVIS:	Yo, it's good luck, now put your arm around my—
BRETT:	OK, it is very late so—
D/ALEXA:	STOP IT!!!
BRETT:	Can we just all keep it down a bit?
D/ALEXA:	PUT ME DOWN!
D/TRAVIS:	Yo, I got you, just shut up for once!
D/ALEXA:	YOU SHUT UP! I'm falling! HELP!!!
BRETT:	*(Saves her, carries her over the threshold.)* OK! I got you. Here we go...
D/ALEXA:	WEEEEE! LOOK AT ME! I'm a princess! You're my knight in shiny armour!
BRETT:	Shhh. Quietly now. Let me show you to your room.
D/TRAVIS:	*(Bitter.)* Sweet.

A small shift. Again, BRETT tip-toes down the hall.

D/CHUCK:	Boo!
BRETT:	Ahh! Chuck, you're still up.

D/CHUCK: We've got to stop meeting like this.

BRETT: Do you need anything?

D/CHUCK: What did you have in mind?

BRETT: *(Uncomfortable laughter.)* Have a good night. *(He starts to go, but—)*

D/CHUCK: Whenever I saw you on telly, I always wondered which team you played for.

BRETT: Well…mystery solved!

D/CHUCK: *(Uncomfortably close.)* Want to know why I was tossing and turning?

B/SYLVIA: *(Appearing suddenly.)* Ahem! Am I interrupting something?

D/CHUCK: Oh! No! We were just…saying good night.

B/SYLVIA: Hmmm…I see… Brett, is it? Could you please speak to the people in the room next to mine? They're making a lot of…

D/TRAVIS: Ohhhhh yeah, baby!

D/ALEXA: YEEEAHH, TRAVIS! YEEEEAAAAHHH!!! *(Continues under…)*

BRETT: *(Knock, knock, knock.)* Hi. HELLO?! I know it's your wedding night, but we do have other guests.

D/TRAVIS & ALEXA: YEAH! OH YEEEEAHHHH! UH! UH! UHHHHHHHHH!!!

BRETT: *(Beat. Beat.)* Have a good sleep.

    Shift.

DREW: Good morning! Who wants coffee? Sylvia?

B/SYLVIA: I should think so. I barely slept a wink.

DREW: Sharon?

B/SHARON: Oh yes please! I slept like a log. Chuck? Hellooo?

D/CHUCK: What? Oh! Coffee. Yes dear.

B/SYLVIA: Something on your mind?

DREW: We won't wait for the other two. I'll be out with breakfast shortly. *(Doorbell!)* But please help yourself to one of these scones. Brett! Can you get that? I'm afraid they might be a bit...homemade.

BRETT: *(Answering door.)* Hey! Chris! Now's not really a good time.

D/CHRIS: I hate to do this to you my lad, but— *(Puppy sounds.)*

BRETT: Oh, no! Hi Rick Mercer! Chris, we'll come and get him on Monday, I promise.

Honking car horn!

D/CHRIS: Brett, I can handle a puppy, and God willing I can handle a baby, but I can't handle both at the same time.

B/ALISON: *(More honking. From the car.)* Sorry! CHRISTINE!? Hurry up!

D/CHRIS: Wish us luck! Be a good lad, Rick Mercer!

B/ALISON: *(More honking.)* Sorry Brett! Now get in the car and drive, woman! UHHHHHHH GOD!

D/TRAVIS & ALEXA: UHHHHHHH GOD! YES! YES! YES!

B/SYLVIA: Sounds like the others are awake.

DREW: And how is everything in here?

B/SYLVIA: We'll need some butter. These scones are hard enough to kill a man.

DREW:	So sorry, excuse me, I'll be right back. *(Goes toward the front door.)*
BRETT:	*(Meeting him.)* Look who's here! *(Puppy sounds.)*
DREW:	Rick Mercer? No! Not now!
BRETT:	Yes, now. Alison's in labour.
D/TRAVIS & ALEXA:	YEAH... OH YEAH...
BRETT:	Are you dealing with that?
DREW:	On my way. Keep him in the kitchen. And keep an eye on the bacon!
BRETT:	Pardon me, everyone. We have a last minute visitor. *(Mercer yaps.)* But he's just going to go back here. *(The kitchen.)*

CHUCK is wheezing and choking.

B/SHARON:	Chuck? Darling? Are you all right?
D/CHUCK:	*(Gasping for breath.)* I...can't...
B/SHARON:	What?
D/CHUCK:	...breathe...
D/TRAVIS & ALEXA:	Ugh! Ugh! UHHHHHH!
DREW:	*(Knock, knock.)* Hey, guys? We're serving breakfast downstairs and we can hear every—
D/TRAVIS & ALEXA:	OOOOOOOOHHHHH!!!!! UUUUUUUHHHHHHHHH!!!!
DREW:	*(Beat. Beat.)* Breakfast is ready!
BRETT:	Now Mercer, you just stay back there like a good boy.

D/CHUCK: *(Still choking.)* Help...me...

B/SHARON: What is it, darling?

D/CHUCK: *(More.)* The...scone...

BRETT: *(Appearing.)* Oh my God! Do you need the Heimlich?

D/CHUCK: Yeah.

BRETT: OK. *(CHUCK bends over, BRETT gives him the Heimlich.)* Is it working?

D/CHUCK: Yeah.

BRETT: Again?

D/CHUCK: Yeah!

BRETT: One.

D/CHUCK: Oh!

BRETT: Two.

D/CHUCK: Yeah!

BRETT: Three.

D/CHUCK: OH YEEEEAAAHHH!!! I mean...cheers, mate.

B/SYLVIA: Does anyone else smell that?

Mercer is barking, having entered the room.

DREW: Rick Mercer, what are you doing in here? *(The smoke detector goes off.)* Brett, I told you to watch the bacon!

BRETT: Oh! Excuse me! I was saving a man's life!

DREW: Rick Mercer, relax. It's just a bit of smoke.

BRETT: No it's not, it's a—

BRETT & DREW:	FIIIIIRE!!!
BRETT:	Call 911!
DREW:	No! Where's the fire extinguisher?!
B/SYLVIA:	Stop it! Bad dog!

The smoke alarm is blaring, Mercer is barking, humping SYLVIA's leg, and now the phone starts ringing.

DREW:	Mercer! OFF!
B/SYLVIA:	You are a very bad boy.
DREW:	*(Extinguishing the fire.)* Brett, can you deal with your dog?
BRETT:	Oh, he's MY dog?
DREW:	I am literally fighting a fire here!
B/SHARON:	You enjoyed that, didn't you Chuck?
D/CHUCK:	Sharon, I...I don't know what you're talking about.
B/SHARON:	Don't play dumb with me, Charles. You haven't enjoyed yourself that much in twenty-five years.
DREW:	*(Answering phone.)* Aunt Maggie's House!
B/SYLVIA:	You're a dirty...
DREW:	Hello?
B/SYLVIA:	Naughty...
DREW:	Hello?
B/SYLVIA:	Nasty boy!
DREW:	*(Hanging up.)* Urrrrgh!

B/SYLVIA: Just like all the rest of them!

D/TRAVIS & ALEXA: *(From upstairs again.)* Oh yeah! Oh yeah! OH YES!

BRETT: I think now would be a good time to offer you all... an apology.

DREW: *(Overlap with "an apology.")* A refund.

Shift. Sounds of a baby crying.

DREW: Oh! She's so tiny.

BRETT: She's beautiful.

D/CHRIS: Yeah, she takes after her mother. That mother, not this mother.

The baby cries a bit more.

B/ALISON: Sorry, Kathleen, shhh, you're OK. Sorry to stick you with Rick Mercer like that! How did your opening weekend go?

DREW: It was...

BRETT: We learned a lot.

DREW: Kathleen's a beautiful name.

BRETT: Is it an old Irish family name, Chris?

D/CHRIS: Hell no. Just because she's a baby doesn't exempt her from the rule.

Shift. To us:

BRETT: "Alison MacMillan and Christine Donnelly are overjoyed to announce the birth of Kathleen Wynne MacMillan-Donnelly—

DREW: "Born May fifth at 3:49 pm. Kathleen and her moms are back home with Anne Murray and k.d. lang and doing well."

BRETT: June.

Shift.

D/CARRIE: Oh my God, Brett, you are never going to believe this.

BRETT: What?

D/CARRIE: I have these new clients. A very nice couple. But they live overseas. They're retiring at the end of the summer and they want to move here and run a B and B. Where were they in September, right? Only they want a place that's ready to go. They came across the pictures on your website and they fell in love with this place.

BRETT: Carrie…what? We just opened. It's not for sale.

D/CARRIE: Oh my God, I know. But they told me what they'd be willing to offer. *(She writes it down.)* It's…this much…

BRETT: *(Looking at it.)* Oh my God.

D/CARRIE: That's exactly what I said! They don't need an answer right away. September first. I know it hasn't been all sunshine and rainbows for you guys, so… it's an option.

BRETT: *(To us.)* Remember how we said we have a decision to make?

DREW: Yeah… That's the one.

BRETT: July.

Shift. Loud music. Doorbell…doorbell…doorbell. CODY answers the door. It's DUSTIN with a box of baking.

B/DUSTIN: Oh! Like hi. Can I just like drop these off in the like kitchen?

D/CODY: I dunno. What are they?

B/DUSTIN: They're like muffins. And like croissants. Brett and Drew like hired me to do the baking for the B and B. They like tried to do it, but I think someone almost like died.

D/CODY: I dunno. These look professional.

B/DUSTIN: Like, I guess. Are you like a guest here?

D/CODY: *(Eating one.)* I dunno. I'm Cody. I'm here for the summer. Working for Doug.

B/DUSTIN: Can you like let them know Dustin dropped these off?

D/CODY: I dunno. This is really good.

B/DUSTIN: Like…thanks. *(Starts to exit, stops.)* Oh and like by the way, I like…like your music.

Shift. The phone rings.

DREW: Aunt Maggie's House, this is Drew. Hello? Who is this? Hello… *(He hangs up.)*

BRETT: *(Entering the scene. Mercer barks.)* Hey, he's getting better on the leash. Who was that?

DREW: Another one of those hang-ups. *(He dials to check the number.)* I can tell someone's there, but— Unlisted. Of course. *(Beat.)* Do you ever look at people and wonder if it was them?

BRETT: What?

DREW: People in town, on the street, at the store. Do you ever think, "Are you the one who did that to our house?"

BRETT: Don't do that, you'll drive yourself crazy.

DREW: They're out there, Brett. Just walking around.

	When I'm out for a run, sometimes I hear "Gay!" yelled from a car window. Or around town, I get these looks from people and I think, "What? What am I doing? Am I standing a certain way? How am I talking? What am I doing with my hands?" I haven't done that since I was a teenager.
BRETT:	After what happened, I can understand. It's OK.
DREW:	No, Brett, it's not! I like to think of myself as this strong, proud gay man, someone who knows better than to fall into that shit—but apparently, I'm not. So yeah, I dug in my heels before Christmas and we didn't run away, but every time we get one of these phone calls, all I can think is someone's checking to see if we're home, planning whatever they're going to do next. And on top of all that, I think, "What am I doing to cause it?" I just— Maybe we should seriously consider taking Carrie up on this offer.
BRETT:	And do what? Go back to Toronto?
DREW:	Even when every room is full, we're not making any money.
BRETT:	*(Beat.)* Do you just want to get away for a couple days? Go visit Ray?
DREW:	We're booked up.
BRETT:	Let me know if we get any more of these calls.
	Shift. DOUG's truck idling, horn honking. Mercer barks. BRETT comes outside.
BRETT:	He'll be out in a minute!
D/DOUG:	He's late. Third time this week. *(Honks the horn.)*
BRETT:	*(Approaching. Mercer barks.)* Mercer, down. Whoa, Doug, what happened to your eye? Were you in a fight?

D/DOUG: Had something to deal with. *(Honk. Bark.)*

BRETT: You know, you can ring the doorbell. You can come inside—you haven't even seen it all finished. *(Honk. Bark.)* Sit. So how's Cody doing?

D/DOUG: Hell of a lot better worker than you ever were.

BRETT: Do you guys take a lunch break? He's eating us out of our home.

D/DOUG: He's eighteen.

BRETT: No, I mean, it's fine. After all those years I stayed with Maggie, I guess it's my turn.

D/DOUG: But...this ain't the same thing.

BRETT: I'm pretty sure it's exactly the same thing, Doug. How is it different?

D/DOUG: Because you— Forget it.

BRETT: Because we're two men you think we can't take care of our nephew? *(Honk. Bark.)* You know, I thought if you spent enough time around me and Drew, you might change. I thought once you got to know us, you wouldn't hate us so much. Guess I was wrong. *(He walks away.)*

DREW: *(To us.)* August.

    Shift.

D/MARTIN: Well son, I'll say one thing: it doesn't look like the house I grew up in.

B/LYNDA: It looks nice, Brett. Not what your father and I would have done, but you two like it and that's what matters. Now tell me, is Cody behaving himself?

DREW: Yes, he's been fine, Lynda. Working hard. He's even made some new friends.

BRETT: Good kids. The boy who does our baking. Nothing to worry about. They're all out at a movie tonight.

D/MARTIN: And what about you, son? Have you been minding your own business?

B/LYNDA: Martin, please.

D/MARTIN: Brett, I uh...I brought something for you. But I'll just...give it to you tomorrow before we go.

Shift.

B/RAY: Oh, girl. This is divine. It's like *Martha Stewart Living* in here, only not so self-righteous. It's post-jail Martha.

DREW: Thanks, Ray. Thank you for coming.

B/RAY: Girl, it's good to see you. So do I have the run of the place?

DREW: No, Brett's parents are here for the night too. They're going to love you. This was one of the only nights we could squeeze you in.

B/RAY: I'm honoured. So how are you? You didn't sound so hot on the phone.

DREW: You were right. It's hard. There are people interested in buying this place. Big money. I think we might take them up on it. Move back.

B/RAY: What? Girl. Do I need to remind you how miserable you two were in Toronto? You remember when I first met you? When you first arrived? You, Little Miss Thing off the bus from One-Horse-Town, Saskatchewan, Population Negative Two Hundred, I thought you were going to die. I always knew you wouldn't last.

DREW: What?

B/RAY: You're a small town boy, Drew. You've been here

less than a year. Change isn't easy. But if you don't change, you just stay the same, and where's the fun in that? Now! What's a girl got to do to get a drink around this joint?

Shift. BRETT and DREW get ready for bed.

DREW: Did your parents get settled in?

BRETT: Once I explained they don't need to sleep with all the pillows. And Ray?

DREW: Two martinis and he was done. That guy used to be fun. Hey, what do you think your dad brought for you?

BRETT: I have no clue. I've given up trying to understand my family. They speak in code.

DREW: Oh, Carrie called again. She wants to know if we've made up our minds about selling.

BRETT: What did you tell her?

DREW: That we still don't know.

BRETT: But it's looking better all the time.

CODY's music, blaring from down the hall.

DREW: Guess who's home!

BRETT: What is he doing? It's after midnight. Can you go talk to him?

DREW: He's your nephew.

BRETT: And yours.

The both go. Outside CODY's door. Very loud music. They knock and whisper-yell.

Cody?

DREW:	CODY! PEOPLE ARE SLEEPING.
BRETT:	*(Knock, knock.)* DO YOU KNOW WHAT TIME IT IS? *(He opens the door.)* What is going on in here?!
D/CODY:	I dunno. I dunno. I DUNNO!
B/DUSTIN:	Like. Oh my God. Like.
DREW:	Dustin! What are you doing!?
B/DUSTIN:	We were just like— We were like—
DREW:	No, I know what you were doing, Dustin. Can you put some clothes on?
BRETT:	Cody, can you turn that off?
D/CODY:	I dunno. *(The music stops.)* OK, this is not what it looks like.
BRETT:	Oh, I'm pretty sure it's exactly what it looks like. We had two rules when you came to live here: keep the music down and no one in your room. What do you have to say for yourself?
D/CODY:	I dunno! But the rule was no girls in my room.
BRETT:	Cody! What, are you gay now?
D/CODY:	I dunno! Dustin started it.
B/DUSTIN:	Like, what!? Like, no I didn't. Like, you did.
DREW:	Seriously, Dustin, put some pants on.
BRETT:	Cody, why didn't you just tell us you're gay?
D/CODY:	I dunno! And who says I'm gay? Why do you keep saying I'm gay?
BRETT:	Because! Of what you were—! That looked very gay! That looked like the definition of gay!
D/CODY:	I dunno! Why are you getting so mad? You're so old-fashioned!

BRETT: I know it can be hard to come to terms with, Cody, but based on what you were doing just now—

D/CODY: I'm eighteen! I'm human! I'm horny! I dunno! We just like each other. So maybe I'm gay or maybe I'm not or I dunno maybe I'm somewhere in between. But maybe I don't have to have that figured out right now! And maybe I don't need to put everything in a little box with a little label! And maybe this isn't Russia or Uganda or Indiana and I dunno maybe I don't feel like I should have to defend myself to my two gay uncles who I thought were supposed to be cool!

BRETT: *(Beat.)* Well then.

D/CODY: I dunno. Please don't tell Grandma and Grandpa. Or my dad.

BRETT: We won't. Just...keep the music down, OK boys?

They close the door.

DREW: Did he just call us old-fashioned?

BRETT: Yeah...

They head back to their room. The phone rings. BRETT starts to go for it, but DREW stops him and answers.

DREW: Hello? Who the hell is this? What do you want? Hello! *(He hangs up.)* Damn it!

Shift. Morning. DOUG's horn honking.

BRETT: Damn it! *(From the door.)* He's coming, OK? He had a late night. *(He starts to go.)*

D/DOUG: I don't hate you, Brett.

BRETT: *(Stops.)* What?

D/DOUG: You said that I— I don't.

BRETT: Whatever, Doug. My mom and dad are here, so I have to go.

D/DOUG: They didn't tell you yet, eh?

BRETT: Tell me what?

D/DOUG: Sons of bitches. Called your dad, told him if he didn't tell you, I would.

BRETT: *(Finally approaching.)* What are you talking about?

D/DOUG: You asked about Maggie's baby.

BRETT: Doug, I dropped that, OK? I—

D/DOUG: I was married to Brenda, but I was young and Maggie was just so… We just—just a couple times, but— We swore we wouldn't tell and uh…

BRETT: Oh my God, are you saying that you're the father?

D/DOUG: But when she died and when you moved out here, I— You know, it took me a while to track 'em down, but I did.

BRETT: Who? The baby?

D/DOUG: No. The people who did it. To this place. Before Christmas.

BRETT: Wait…you know who it was? Did you call the police?

D/DOUG: I took care of it, all right? You think that black eye was bad, you should see them.

BRETT: What are you talking about?

D/DOUG: I just… I couldn't let something like that happen to my own flesh and blood.

BRETT: I don't understand…

D/DOUG: When's your birthday, Brett?

BRETT:	November. Fourteenth.
D/DOUG:	Not too long after Halloween. *(Beat.)* Took me a while, but I tracked 'em down. Nobody does that to my son.
BRETT:	I uh... I... I... *(He goes back inside.)* Mom, Dad, get in here. Now.

Shift.

D/MARTIN:	We thought we were doing the right thing, son.
B/LYNDA:	We wanted a little brother for Steven. And I was... but I miscarried and uh...at the same time...
D/MARTIN:	Maggie was in trouble.
B/LYNDA:	But she still got to see you grow up.
D/MARTIN:	Everyone agreed it would be easier if we kept it a uh...
B/LYNDA:	We just...we didn't want to lose you, Brett.

Shift.

DREW:	Oh, sweetie. I always knew your family kept it all bottled up, but this is... *(An exhalation or vocalization of disbelief.)*
BRETT:	How can we keep living here if everything in this place has been one big lie?
DREW:	We don't have to. We can leave. Your uh... Martin said this is for you. *(A letter.)* This is what he was going to give you today before they left, but it sounds like Doug beat him to the punch. You were supposed to get it when Maggie died, but your parents chose to...
BRETT:	It was written almost nine years ago. *(He reads. Partway through, a gradual, magical, spiritual shift happens and BRETT transforms into MAGGIE.)*

Dear Brett. I'm on my way back home from visiting you in Toronto. On the train. So that explains my messy handwriting. Plus I've had a couple of VIA Rail white wines. Liquid courage, eh? Hey! This new Drew fella is a catch! Hang on to that one. So…I've had two friends my age drop dead in the past six months and that got me thinking. Uh-oh, eh? I hope I live to be ninety-five. I hope you're old and grey yourself when you're reading this and everything in here is old, boring news. I hope between now and the time I kick the bucket, I finally grow a pair and tell you to your face. But just in case…I want you to know… I'm your mom. Surprise! I wanted to tell you the summer you were eighteen, but you had enough of your own stuff going on and your mom and dad and everybody in the whole wide world told me I should still shut up and be ashamed and whaddaya know, I listened to 'em. And that weighs on me every day. Shame… what a stupid, ugly, useless thing that is, eh? Lots of folks think you should be ashamed too. But you just keep living your life, all right? You flip 'em all the bird just by living your life. So. I have a meeting to make a will this week. I'm going to throw this letter in there, just in case. And I decided I'm gonna leave you the house. We spent a lot of good times there, you and me, some of the happiest times of my life. Do whatever you want with the old joint. I leave it to you, my boy. And if neither of us screwed things up too bad down here, I'll see you up there on the other side. Love you forever. *(Back as himself.)* Maggie.

Shift. To us:

DREW: So. That is the full story. How we got here.

BRETT: Well…just about. Earlier today.

Shift. Mercer is barking.

D/CHRIS: *(Throws a ball.)* Go get it, Mercer. Get the ball. It's over there. *(Mercer is hopeless.)* Anybody need another beer?

B/ALISON: *(Breastfeeding.)* Sorry! Yes! Ow! Sorry. I'll have another one.

D/CHRIS: Slow down, woman. At this rate, Kathleen'll be sucking beer straight from your tit.

B/ALISON: Sorry, it helps her sleep. Give me that.

D/CHRIS: *(Mercer got the ball.)* Well, would you look at that! Good dog!

BRETT: Hey Cody, you want another burger before you go?

D/CODY: I dunno. No thanks.

BRETT: Did you just say no to food? Are you OK?

D/CODY: I dunno. *(Sound of DOUG's truck.)* Sounds like Doug's here, so...

BRETT: Is he driving you all the way to school?

D/CODY: I dunno. My Dad's taking the rest of my stuff from his house and meeting us there.

BRETT: Did you check your room one last time? *(Walking away.)* We don't need any more surprises.

B/DUSTIN: *(Approaching.)* Hey Codester. Do you like want a cookie for the road?

D/CODY: I dunno. OK.

   Mercer barks...and humps DOUG's leg as he arrives.

D/DOUG: You little son of a bitch, cut that out. Hey kid, you ready to hit the road?

D/CODY: I dunno. I mean... Yes. I'm ready. Thanks, Uncle Brett. Thanks, Uncle Drew. OK. So. *(To DUSTIN.)* Bye.

B/DUSTIN: Like...bye.

CODY walks away, but stops. Beat. He turns back to DUSTIN and plants a big kiss on him.

D/CODY: Thanks for the cookie, Dustinator. *(He walks away.)*

D/DOUG: Oh yeah. Well. *(He laughs for the first time.)* Son of a bitch!

The phone rings.

DREW: I got it. *(He goes inside, answers.)* Hello, Aunt Maggie's House, Drew speaking. Hello? OK, what do we have to say to make ourselves clear?

B/VOICE: Drew?

DREW: Uh yes, sorry, this is Drew. Who's this?

B/VOICE: Andrew? Lazarenko?

DREW: Speaking.

B/VOICE: We...we got your Christmas card, so I knew where you were at...

DREW: ...Hi.

B/VOICE: Your mother's just in the other room and she's still not— So I can't— But it's good to hear your voice.

DREW: Yeah. You too. Thanks for calling, Dad.

Beat. Click. Dial tone. Shift. To us:

BRETT: There. Up to the present. One year to the day from where we started. And so... *(To DREW.)* Now what?

DREW: Tomorrow is September. Carrie really needs an answer.

BRETT: I know. What do you say?

DREW: If you had asked me a year ago what we wanted, I would have said we wanted a house. And we got one. But we were wrong, Brett. A house is just four walls and a roof, you know? With the amount of money those people are offering, we could get ourselves a house anywhere. But a home... A home is people. Home is where your people are. I think that's what we wanted. And that's what we got. Can we... Can we stay here?

BRETT: Yes. Yes! Let's stay here.

DREW: I'll call Carrie in the morning and let her know.

A shift has slowly occurred. BRETT and DREW now undress for bed.

BRETT: Remember that big group checks in early tomorrow.

DREW: I remember. I can handle it. Take all the design jobs you can get.

BRETT: It's not really a design job—Doug just needs help picking out tile.

DREW: Still...he's paying you.

BRETT: *(Beat.)* So...do you think those calls have been your dad all along?

DREW: I think so? God, I hope so. Maybe I can ask him someday. *(Beat. They undress.)* When he built this place, do you think great-great grandpa could have ever imagined that bunch of queers in his backyard? Two of them his own flesh and blood? What would he have to say about that?

BRETT: Maybe he would have wanted to join us. Or maybe the Rumrunner...he never married, you never know! I mean, maybe we've always been here: you and me, Alison and Chris, Dustin...Cody? Maybe these closets have been packed so full with so many secrets for so long...Maggie, Doug. Maybe we're lucky to be alive when the doors can bust open... you know what I mean?

DREW: I do. *(He's in bed. Beat.)* Hey Mister. You coming to bed?

BRETT nods. He climbs into bed. In the glow of the bedside lamps, they kiss. They kiss again. The kissing grows more and more intense...

Blackout.

The End.

Likewise

Whereas

In addition to / Additionally

Similarly

However

Moreover

In spite of

Alternatively

Following

Unlike

As well as

In particular

Generally

In order to

Above all

Prior to

Previously

Nevertheless